Cowley Publications is a ministry of the brothers of the Society of Saint John the Evangelist, a monastic order in the Episcopal Church. Our mission is to provide books and resources for those seeking spiritual and theological formation. Cowley Publications is committed to developing a new generation of writers and teachers who will encourage people to think and pray in new ways about spirituality, reconciliation, and the future.

DEEP PEACE:
HEALING IN OUR LIVES

Deep Peace: Healing in Our Lives

J. Ellen Nunnally

Published in the United States of America by Cowley Publications, a
division of the Society of Saint John the Evangelist. No portion of this book
may be reproduced, stored in or introduced into a retrieval system, or
transmitted, in any form or by any means—including photocopying—without
the prior written permission of Cowley Publications, except in the case of
brief quotations embedded in critical articles and reviews.

Library of Congress Cataloging-in-Publication Data:
Nunnally, J. Ellen, 1945-
  Deep peace : healing in our lives / J. Ellen Nunnally.
      p. cm.
Includes bibliographical references and index.
  ISBN 1-56101-219-X (alk. paper)
    1. Christian life—Anglican authors. 2. Peace—Religious aspects—
Episcopal Church. 3. Healing—Religious aspects—Episcopal Church. I. Title.
  BV4647.P35N86 2003
    234'.131—dc21   2003013169

Scripture quotations are taken from *The New Revised Standard Version of the
Bible*, © 1989, by the Division of Christian Education of the National Council
of the Churches of Christ in the United States of America. Used by permission.

Cover art: An early 20th Century Pilkington tile depicting water lily, buds
and pads. Machine impressed and decorated in translucent blue, green
and yellow glazes. Courtesy Taggart Gallery, Great Staughton, England
(www.taggartgallery.co.uk). Reproduced with permission. All rights reserved.

Cover design: Kevin R. Hackett and Jennifer Hopcroft

This book was printed on acid-free paper.

COWLEY PUBLICATIONS
907 Massachusetts Avenue
Cambridge, Massachusetts 02139
800-225-1534 • www.cowley.org

CONTENTS

FOREWORD

Perhaps my own longing for peace is what first brought me Ellen Nunnally's friendship and now her book, *Deep Peace*. She puts me in mind of the psalmist's cry:

> *Too long have I had my dwelling*
> *among those who hate peace.*
> *I am for peace,*
> *but when I speak, they are for war.*
> *(Ps. 120:6, 7)*

The magnitude of these words breaks in on us daily. Peace and peacemaking can no longer remain on the second rung of our Christian conscience. There is too much talk of war. There are too many enemies of peace.

In language emerging from her own experience and formation, Ellen takes us down a road toward peace, a road marked by story, prayer, and "the hard part": her sound, hallowed advice asking us to respond to many invitations. The road is hard only if we resist. She stops at various places along the way, staying for a while, and asks us to come along. Ellen explores and sings, interprets and teaches, holds us close to God and sets us free to go to God in our own ways. And she gives us signposts.

At one point on the journey, Ellen asks us to stop at her grandmother's nineteenth-century farmhouse on the Western Reserve in Ohio. The house is warm and inviting, and outside are the sounds and sights of God's creation. This will be a safe place, she tells us, although we already know the truth of it because she has taken us there. The birds, the grasses and flowers and ponds, remind us of our own safe places. Ellen calls them places of the heart.

That is where this book takes us, to places of the heart: the heart of God discovered in scripture, prayer, and the blessing found in the simplicity and loveliness of every day. When we abide in the heart of God, we are given God's peace. This truth of God's peace has to be spoken, and Ellen has done that in a most compelling way. However, witness alone is not enough. The truth of peace has to be lived: courageously, intelligently, prayerfully, gently, lovingly, and unceasingly.

This is a book that tells us how. Come along. *Deep Peace* has some things to show us.

THE RT. REV. J. CLARK GREW II
BISHOP OF OHIO

Ho, everyone who thirsts,
come to the waters!
(Isa. 55:1)

PREFACE

In our first conversation, my gifted editor asked a simple question: what was the inception of *Deep Peace*? Was it my idea, or Cowley's? I had to think about that. I didn't know Cowley, and Cowley didn't know me when I presented them with the idea of this book. But then again, was it my idea, or the Spirit's? I've been carrying these thoughts in my head for a long time. In the early days of women priests, when we couldn't get hired, I ran from parish to parish in Washington, D.C., teaching *Foremothers*, my previous book. After I did that long enough, I started to teach a series on the biblical healing stories: wonderful stories of forgiveness, freedom, acceptance, kindness and mercy, joy. Healing, and the need for healing, seemed to be so central in my own life and the lives of those I met. These small stories spoke to that kind of transformation. From this beginning came the first part of this book, "Healing Stories."

The second part, "Healing Prayer," emerged from my own prayer evolution over the years, and from my long association with the Shalem Institute for Spiritual Formation. I graduated from Virginia Theological Seminary twice; the first time around I wrote a thesis on active and contemplative prayer. I knelt in the chapel every morning and said several cycles of prayer. But I didn't know much about silence until I discovered Shalem, during my second round of seminary. I joined a group of twenty-five people, of varying faiths or no faith, at one of the religious houses near Catholic University. We sat on the floor together from fall through spring, and experienced silence as well as various forms of silent prayer. My experience of this meditative prayer grew over time, as did my understanding of the deep healing that this prayer brings when practiced.

The third part, "Healing Practice," is something I have not taught nor even articulated until now. The last section alone, on practicing peace, could probably be a book in itself. But there is more than this to healing practice, which aims to rediscover many things we've lost amid the bustle of modern life: the rhythm of monastic hours, the making of a rule of life, life in the Spirit, sabbath time, and finally, practicing peace. All of these last topics form a larger design, quilt pieces sewn together to make a whole. For it seems to me that such connections are what we're looking for now: for healing, that wholeness or holy practice that will sustain us through these terrible times. The events of September 11, 2001 have wrought in us a new image of pain: we can be people of peace, or people of war, and perhaps there is no middle ground. But before we can become people of peace, we have to find healing in our own lives.

In this respect, *Deep Peace* is a practical book. It is also an experience, however. You can pick and choose whatever will help, whatever will guide, whatever will inspire, to take you down to the river of God's peace. The river runs deep beneath our lives and gives us the strength, the courage, and the vision to carry on. In John's gospel, Jesus asks the man at the Sheep Gate Pool if he wants to be healed. Like that man, all we have to do is say: *yes.*

THE REV. J. ELLEN NUNNALLY
DIOCESE OF WASHINGTON
WINTER 2003

ACKNOWLEDGMENTS

I'm grateful to many who have cared for me, over the years. With thanks to Kevin R. Hackett ssje and the brothers of the Society of Saint John the Evangelist for their enthusiasm and interest, and to Susan Brown for her editing and friendship. For Sid, Jesse, David, and Milton, my seminary professors; for Jerry, Joan, Darlene, and Peggy of Shalem Institute; for Rhoda, Connie, and Lorene for years of prayers; and for Carol and Sally, my counselors through dark times. With thanks to the Dioceses of Washington and Ohio for education funds, and with special thanks to the Rev. Larry Harris, who believed in me, and the Bishop of Ohio, Clark Grew, for his friendship and great kindness.

For Alanon friends and others who helped me through: Beth, Clyde, Pat, and Bobby in Virginia; Connie, John, Susie, Sue, Sarah, Deleasa, and Judy in Ohio; and for the saving grace of my mother Harriet, Aunt Alice, and Elizabeth. For the Rev. Jerry Flora's friendship, and for the hospitality of St. Matthew's, Ashland, and Grace Church, Galion. For the steady support of cousin Phyllis, brother Dave, and uncle Frank, and for cousin Todd who lights up my life. For the continuing prayers of St. Helena's Convent. And for my family in Virginia and Ohio: Holly and Anna; Forrest and Harriet; and Sam, Honey, and the cats. I love you all, and am grateful each waking day.

Deep peace of the *running wave* to you
deep peace of the *flowing air* to you
deep peace of the *quiet earth* to you
deep peace of the *shining stars* to you
deep peace of the *Son of Peace* to you.

OLD SCOTTISH BLESSING
ISLE OF IONA

In thanksgiving
for my home
and family.

And wherever he went, into villages or cities or farms,
they laid the sick in the marketplaces, and begged him
that they might touch even the fringe of his cloak;
and all who touched it were healed.
(Mk 6:56)

I. HEALING STORIES

The healing stories of Jesus and the people he meets are a powerful
force in the New Testament gospels. Morton Kelsey tells us, in his
classic *Healing and Christianity*, that "nearly one-fifth of the entire
gospels is devoted to Jesus' healing and the discussions occasioned
by it" (42). This figure includes physical and mental healings, but
does not include what Kelsey calls "moral healings," or what I myself would call "soul healing": stories like the woman at the well,
the woman anointing, or tax collector Zacchaeus in the tree.
Whether the healings are physical, mental, or emotional, one
cannot read these gospel stories without being confronted with startling truths. Something happened to all these people; their lives
were turned around. Like the wise men in Matthew's gospel, they
ended up going home by another way.

That Jesus functioned as a religious healer is clearer than anything
else in the gospels. That he sent his followers out to continue this
healing ministry is also clear (Mk 6:7–13; Mt 10:1, 5–10; Lk 9:1–6).
The healing stories stand like beacons of light among the other stories and biblical instruction. But a number of scholars today, including

Robert Funk of the Jesus Seminar and Anglican Bishop John Spong, argue that the healing stories simply never happened, that they are part of a supernatural theistic package of virgin birth-miracles-resurrection-ascension stories, that is no longer viable or believable.

Be that as it may, I like to think of the healing stories as not only possible, but powerfully possible, despite the theistic layering they have collected over the centuries. Did Jesus lay his hands on people and heal them? It seems that way. There is a kernel of Truth hidden away in these stories, shining like a diamond, something we can't ignore. I simply suggest reading the stories with an open heart and open mind: visualize them, if possible, see and smell them, experience them and translate them for yourself. What is true here? What abides? What in them is strong enough to remain and speak to our own lives today?

So let's get started. Let's dive into an old, deep well. We may not be able to view all the healing stories, but we'll look at some. You'll need a good Bible, something readable, preferably not the *King James* version. The King James language is beautiful, but not understandable. Even the *Revised Standard Version* has been revised. Now we have the *New Revised Standard Version (NRSV)*. We also have the *New American Bible, (NAB)*, the *New Jerusalem Bible (NJB)*, the *New International Version (NIV)*, and the *Revised English Bible (REB)*, formerly the *New English Bible*. All of these Bibles were revised in the 1980s and 1990s, except the *NIV*, the most conservative translation. In addition we have paraphrased translations from earlier years, The *Good News Bible* and the *Living Bible (LB)*. Scholar Raymond E. Brown cautions, however, that the *LB* holds many translation errors. Any of the above will work, though, according to your preferences. Look at several versions, and try them out!

My own choice is the *New Oxford Annotated Bible with the Apocrypha (NRSV)*, an ecumenical study Bible. The footnotes are wonderful; an education in themselves. But if you want something a little less technical, the *REB* and *NJB* are also solid versions. Once you have made a choice, get out your markers and prepare to 'read, mark, and inwardly digest.' If you've never read the biblical stories, you have a treasury of multicolored pearls waiting. What a reading treat!

Our healing stories appear in four books, *Matthew, Mark, Luke,* and *John,* called the canonical (from 'measuring rod' or 'rule') gospels. Several other gospels are not accepted as canon by the church, including the gospels of Mary, Peter, Philip, and Thomas. But for our purposes, we'll be reading from the gospels that had become canon by 200 CE The New Testament canon eventually came to include these four gospels, the Acts of the Apostles, thirteen letters by or attributed to Paul, and other writings. Within the gospel canon, we'll now take a look at five types of healing stories: *transformation stories, Sabbath stories, stories of foreigners and outcasts, friends' stories,* and *death stories.*

⚜ 1 ⚜

Transformation Stories

The New Testament holds a number of transformation stories, in which people find themselves dramatically changed, including Saul (Paul), who has a blinding vision (Acts 9), and Cornelius the centurion, who sees a vision of an angel (Acts 10). Both men experience conversion and come to follow Jesus. Several stories in the gospels address healings of the inner self: people in need of forgiveness or acceptance find themselves suddenly transformed in encounters with Jesus. Let's now take a look at four of these stories: a woman anointing, Zacchaeus in the tree, a woman drawing water, and a woman in the temple courtyard.

A Woman Anointing
(Lk 7:36–50; Mt 26:6–13; Mk 14:3–9; Jn 12:1–8)

Let's start with the woman who anoints Jesus, one of my personal favorites. This woman's story appears in all four gospels, and shapeshifts as it goes; details, places, and people change, but the central story stays the same. Let's call the woman Susanna, to give her a name. In Luke's version of the story, the setting is a dinner party at a Pharisee's house, probably in Jerusalem. Susanna is described as "a woman in the city, who was a sinner." She brings an alabaster jar of ointment, very costly, and stands behind Jesus, weeping. Jesus is reclined at table, with his feet stretched out on a couch: Susanna bathes his feet with her tears and dries them with her long hair. The sweet scent of her oil drifts through the house.

But Simon the Pharisee is disturbed. He tells himself that if Jesus were indeed a prophet, he would know the kind of woman touching him. Jesus responds to the Pharisee's inward thoughts with *"Simon, I have something to say to you."* He tells a story about a creditor who canceled the debts of two debtors. Jesus asks Simon who will love the creditor more, the man who owes more money, or the one who owes less. Jesus then scolds the Pharisee for not being a better host; he has given no water for Jesus' feet, no kiss of greeting, no oil of anointing for his head. Jesus says that the woman's sins, which are many, are now forgiven. He turns to her and says: *"Your sins are forgiven. . .your faith has saved you, go in peace."* In that one moment, Susanna's life is entirely changed.

In all four versions of this story, regardless of the particular details, a lot of *conflict* is going on. The guests/host are not happy with the intrusion of the woman on their meal, with her anointing Jesus, or with the cost of the oil/perfume. To them she is a nuisance. Imagine how Susanna must have felt, when Jesus tells her she is forgiven. We don't know her burdens, but they must have been many: she weeps profusely, bathing Jesus' feet with her tears. In Luke's story, Susanna doesn't even feel worthy to anoint Jesus' head. But in an instant, in one scene at a dinner party, her life finds blessed healing. She leaves the guests and host behind and goes in peace to a new life.

Zacchaeus
(Lk 19:1–10)

Others also have such moments of transformation when they feel acceptable despite their reputations. One of these is Zacchaeus, in the gospel of Luke. Zacchaeus is a "chief tax collector and. . .rich."

In the story Jesus enters Jericho, an important customs center on a main trade route. Jesus' arrival attracts a great crowd, and Zacchaeus tries to catch sight of him; he is "short in stature," so he climbs a large sycamore tree for a better view. When Jesus and the crowd pass by the sycamore, Jesus stops, looks up, and says: *"Zacchaeus, hurry and come down; for I must stay at your house today."* An amazed Zacchaeus climbs down to welcome his new guest.

But not all are pleased with the meeting, and some "grumble," calling Zacchaeus a sinner. The tax collector, not to be undone, says to Jesus: *"Look, half of my possessions, Lord, I will give to the poor."* He further says if he has defrauded "anyone of anything" he will pay that person back four times over. Jesus pays him a high compliment, saying: *"Today salvation has come to this house."* He calls Zacchaeus a "son of Abraham," an esteemed title.

This is a radical story, precisely because of the ending act of grace. Zacchaeus is not just a tax collector; he is the *chief* tax collector for the Romans, and a very wealthy man. The neighbors in his district would have despised him for foreign collaboration: to them he would have been ceremonially unclean, a sinner, and a political traitor. He would have been shunned by the Jews, his own people. But deep healing takes place in the life and home of this man. Zacchaeus feels forgiven. He is even willing to give half his possessions to the poor. We can only imagine the peace that entered Zacchaeus's heart on the day he climbed the sycamore tree.

A Woman Drawing Water
(Jn 4:1–42)

Like Susanna and Zacchaeus, the woman at the well has a day when her life is transformed. She's a Samaritan, one of those held in contempt by Jews as "half-breeds" and religious apostates. Her town is Sychar, and she collects water from the well of Jacob. Let's call her Asa. The story begins with Jesus and his disciples in the southern territory of Judea. Jesus hears that the Pharisees, hostile to John the Baptist, are now turning on Jesus and his followers. He wants to find safety at home in northern Galilee, so instead of traveling around Samaria, as Jews would do, he goes straight through. Jesus is tired from his journey and sits down by Jacob's well. It's noontime, and hot.

The disciples have gone into town to buy food, when Asa walks out to draw water. At the well, Jesus asks her for a drink. She is surprised he speaks to her at all: "How is it that you, a Jew, ask a drink of me, a woman of Samaria?" Jesus speaks to her of many things, including "living water." Asa is confused and responds by saying: "Sir, you have no bucket, and the well is deep. Where do you get that living water?" She asks Jesus to give her this water, so she can never be thirsty again and can stop coming to draw water from the well.

But Jesus changes the subject to her husbands. Asa has had five husbands and is living with yet another man. She doesn't offer this information, but Jesus sees it through her. She changes the subject again: "Sir, I see that you are a prophet." Their conversation is then interrupted by the returning disciples, who are "astonished" that Jesus speaks with a woman, especially a woman of Samaria. An elated Asa runs all the way back to Sychar, leaving her water jar behind. "Come and see," she says to the people, "a man who told me everything I have ever done!"

Asa's story is so touching. She starts out being afraid of a stranger, yet he, a Jew, drinks from her own jar and they talk. In the end, she runs off in such excitement that she leaves the water jar behind. For once in her life, someone has seen her so clearly that she is able to see herself. Asa has lived with a number of husbands, gone from one man to another, perhaps hoping for some kind of peace or stability. On this day, Jesus has given her "living water" to drink, and her life is transformed and changed. She finds peace, and the town welcomes Jesus and his followers.

A Woman in the Temple Courtyard
(Jn 7:53–8:11)

Another story in John's gospel describes a transformational time, during early morning at the great Temple in Jerusalem. A woman is "caught in adultery;" again she is a nameless figure, so let's call her Hannah. In the opening scene Jesus comes early to the Temple, having spent the night at the Mount of Olives. "All the people come to him," and he teaches in the courtyard, where women and men are able to mix. Scribes and Pharisees, Jewish rulers, bring in Hannah. They force her to stand before all of them, then question Jesus about the Law of Moses. "Moses," they say, "commanded us to stone such women. Now what do you say?"

Jesus says nothing. In the flurry of accusation around him, he bends down and "writes with his finger on the ground." He says: "Let anyone among you who is without sin be the first to throw a stone at her." Then he bends and continues to write in the dust. One by one the rulers slip away, beginning with the elders. Jesus is left alone with Hannah. He speaks to her: "Woman, where are they? Has no one condemned you?" "No one," she says. Jesus says he does not condemn her, and tells her to go her way. "From now on," he says, "do not sin again."

This is truly an astounding story. In our twenty-first century, we cannot begin to understand the extent of ancient Jewish law condemning adultery. Adulterers were stoned to death, or made to drink a "water of bitterness" causing them to become deathly ill (Lev 20:10; Num 5:20–22; Deut 22:22, 23). Jesus and Hannah would have been familiar with these laws of Moses. Yet in an instant, Hannah is freed. Against all odds and great prejudice, her sins have been forgiven. Hannah will have peace in her heart, a deep peace, borne of the mercy of forgiveness.

The transformation stories belonging to Susanna, Zacchaeus, Asa, and Hannah speak of healings of the heart. These people all experience true *forgiveness* in their lives. They're touched by the strength of love. We don't know the end of their journeys, but we can clearly see the day their worlds changed. We don't know the ends of our own journeys, either, but we can see in these stories the power of forgiveness—whether we're the ones in need of forgiveness, or whether we ourselves need to forgive. These stories are not without conflict or intolerance, but what wins out is something greater: the gift of love and the promise of peace.

⚜ 2 ⚜

Sabbath Stories

Stories equally compelling in the gospels are Sabbath stories, small tales of *freedom:* freedom from the law, freedom from disease, freedom from fear and past tradition. The Jewish people valued above all else the Sabbath, that time from sundown Friday to sundown Saturday when nothing should be done. Sabbath was a time for refreshment, the seventh day, when God "caught breath," and rested from the work of creation. This time for the Jews became a matter of law: no work was to be done, however small.

In Mark 2:23–28 (Mt 12:1–8; Lk 6:1–5), for instance, Jesus and his followers are walking through grain fields on the Sabbath, and they're hungry. The disciples pluck heads of grain, rub them in their hands, and eat them. Some Pharisees who appear to be traveling along say to Jesus: "Look, why are they doing what is not lawful on the Sabbath?" Jesus responds by saying that the Sabbath was made for humans, not humans for the Sabbath. "The Son of Man, he says," is "lord even of the Sabbath."

This attitude causes Jesus trouble, as he regularly champions people over the confines of the Jewish law. Morton Kelsey characterizes Jesus as "fully human, living among down-trodden men and women in an occupied country" (51). And Ben Witherington III, in *The Jesus Quest*, gives us a picture of Jesus' world:

> The image of a gentle Jesus, meek and mild, going about Galilee offering entertaining stories called parables or engaging in abstract academic debates about various religious notions fails to convey the sensitive and sometimes hostile atmosphere in which Jesus operated and the *effect* his teaching would have on those who lived in this environment. It was an atmosphere in which politics and religion were almost always mixed. (16)

Let us look, then, at five Sabbath stories recorded in the gospels and their themes of great *freedom*: a man with a withered hand, a woman with a spirit, a man who had dropsy, a man at the Sheep Gate Pool, and a man blind from birth.

A Man with a Withered Hand
(Mk 3:1–6, Mt 12: 9–14, Lk 6: 6–11)

Following the story of the disciples in the field, we find a small healing story of "a man. . .who had a withered hand." The time is once again the Sabbath, and the place is a synagogue. Let's call this man Silas. And let's imagine a simple man from the country, one who has worked hard all his life in the fields. His hand was crippled long ago, but he still attends synagogue and says his prayers, as his parents did before him. He's not expecting anything unusual to happen on this particular day. He's thus surprised to see a new young prophet in his place of worship, and even more surprised when he himself becomes the center of attention.

In Mark's gospel, Jesus tells Silas to "come forward." Then he asks the question: "Is it lawful to do good or to do harm on the Sabbath, to save life or to kill?" In Matthew's gospel, the same question is turned on Jesus, by Pharisees and those present: "Is it lawful to cure on the Sabbath?" Jesus responds with a story: if you have only one sheep, and it falls into a pit on the Sabbath, won't you pull it out? In the middle of this conflict Jesus gives Silas a simple, clear command: "Stretch out your hand." Silas does, and his hand is restored to its natural shape. But Jesus is still angry with the Pharisees, for their "hardness of heart" (Mark), and the scribes and Pharisees are "filled with fury" (Luke) over the healing. The story tells us they conspired with others about how to destroy Jesus.

Silas and his withered hand get lost in this little tale of intrigue, politics, and power. We hear more of the rulers than we do of Silas himself. Yet there is his hand: healed and whole. Fear he must have felt, yes, but freedom, too—for he sees the Sabbath laws come tumbling down for one simple man sitting in a synagogue. Silas can now build again, eat again, play again, control a team of mules: all because of extraordinary grace, on an ordinary Sabbath day.

A Woman with a Spirit
(Lk. 13:10–17)

The gospel of Luke holds an equally powerful small story. In chapter 13, we hear of a crippled woman. Jesus is teaching in one of the synagogues, again on the Sabbath. A woman appears "with a spirit that had crippled her for eighteen years." The woman, let's call her Delilah, is bent over and unable to stand up straight. Jesus sees her, calls to her, and says something that will change her life forever: "Woman, you are set free from your ailment." He places his hands on her, and she stands straight, praising God. Delilah has not even asked for this; she is simply part of the crowds of people gathering around.

But the story doesn't end there: the Jewish synagogue leader is greatly disturbed that Sabbath laws have just been broken, and he wants the crowd to be gone. There are six days to do work in, he says: come on those days and be healed. He and Jesus get into a shouting match. You hypocrites! Jesus says; each of you unties your ox or donkey on the Sabbath to give it water. And ought not this woman, a daughter of Abraham, bound by Satan for eighteen long years, be set free from bondage? Jesus' opponents are put to shame, and the crowd rejoices.

Eighteen long years: imagine how Delilah must feel on her day of freedom. She has looked at the ground so long, she has no idea of the sky. Besides this, the people of her time, including Jesus, believe her body to be inhabited by a "spirit" which causes her to be bent doubled. In their eyes, she's filled with a demon. Yet Jesus calls Delilah, touches her, and gives her a new and honorable name: *daughter of Abraham*. She no longer stands outside the gate, alone, but is part of a community again. Delilah must know deep peace on her day of standing straight. She is free from the shame of her crippled body, and gives loud thanks to God.

A Man who had Dropsy
(Lk 14: 1–6)

Despite the strength of the law, Jesus continues his Sabbath healings. Luke 14 records another small Sabbath story, that of a man who had "dropsy," what we would call swelling from fluid retention. Let's call the man Simon. We have no idea why Simon is present in this story. Perhaps he's been with a crowd, following Jesus. Jesus is once again a dinner guest of a leading Pharisee; it's the Sabbath, and "they were watching him closely." Simon appears out of nowhere. Perhaps family members have brought him, hoping to find healing for his painful swelling.

Jesus says to the gathered lawyers and Pharisees: "Is it lawful to cure people on the Sabbath, or not?" The guests say nothing. Jesus then takes Simon away from the meal, heals him, and sends him on his way. Jesus returns to the dinner party and asks a question: If one of you has a child or ox that has fallen into a well, won't you immediately pull it out—even on a Sabbath day? The guests cannot reply.

Setting is important in this story: it mentions that the guests are choosing "places of honor" at the Pharisee's home. This man is a religious leader, most likely a civic leader as well. This is not, then, just an informal get-together in a peasant's country house, and Simon is clearly not an invited guest. The entire scene is an embarrassment for the Jews, gathered to listen to Jesus and have a nice meal. But Jesus turns this small world upside-down again, by breaking the law. The guests keep their comments to themselves, but anger must be close to the surface. Simon's healing on the Sabbath is unwelcome, but breaking the law in this way has set Simon free.

A Man at the Sheep Gate Pool
(Jn 5:1–18)

Let's look now at two more Sabbath stories from the gospel of John. Our first story opens in Jerusalem, near the Sheep Gate Pool. Old Jerusalem had many gates and pools; the pool in this story is called Beth-zatha and has five porticoes, or porches and walkways with columned roofs. The walkways lead to the pool, and on the porches are a number of invalids—the blind, the lame, and the paralyzed. One man has been there longer than most, for thirty-eight years. Let's call this man Samuel. Jesus comes to the pool on the Sabbath, sees Samuel, and knows he's been there a long time. He goes over to him and asks a simple question: "Do you want to be made well?"

The story tells us that the disabled people await the stirring of the water by an angel. An angel of the Lord comes during certain seasons, and whoever steps in the water first, after the stirrings, is made well. So Samuel tells Jesus that he has no one to help him to the pool when the water ripples, and when he does try to make his way, others rush in and "step down" before him. Jesus says to Samuel: "Stand up, take your mat and walk." Samuel lifts up his mat and walks.

Jews who are present at the scene are not pleased. They stop Samuel and say: "It is the Sabbath; it is not lawful for you to carry your mat." Samuel defends himself by saying that the man who made him well told him to carry his mat and walk. The Jews want to know who this man is, but Jesus has disappeared, and Samuel doesn't know him. He hasn't asked for this, the whole thing has taken him by surprise, and now he's caught by his fellow Jews.

Jesus and Samuel meet up again in the Temple and Jesus says: "Do not sin any more, so that nothing worse happens to you." Samuel then reports Jesus to the Jews. They now are "seeking all the more to kill him," as Jesus calls God "his own Father" and makes himself equal to God. Samuel, in the meantime, has vanished. Will he remember the man who met him by the pool and took the place of angels? Sabbath law, politics, and power overshadow the miraculous end of thirty-eight years of suffering. Samuel is a victim of paralysis and of his time; he does Jesus no favors, but he's still the recipient of radical grace. The gift is given, and Samuel is free.

A Man Blind from Birth
(Jn 9:1–41)

Another story of radical grace and freedom on the Sabbath appears in John: the man born blind. This is a long story, and as John's gospel is based on a number of "signs," this is the *sign of light*. Bread, water, light, life, shepherd, door: these are John's signs. We see water at the wedding in Cana (ch. 2), with the woman at the well (ch. 4), and with the lame man at the pool (ch. 5); we see bread in the feeding of the five thousand (ch. 6). Then, in chapter 9, we hear the disciples ask: "Rabbi, who sinned, this man or his parents, that he was born blind?"

Let's call the blind man Michael. Jesus tells his disciples that no one has sinned: rather, Michael was born blind "so that God's works might be revealed in him." Jesus then spits on the ground, makes mud, spreads the mud on Michael's eyes, and tells him to wash in the pool of Siloam. Michael goes to the pool, washes, and comes back seeing. His neighbors are astonished: "Is this not the man who used to sit and beg?" A dispute follows with Michael telling them yes, "I am the man." Jesus disappears again, and in another scene Michael is taken before the Pharisees.

The following scenes describe heated conversations among Pharisees, Michael, and his parents. The Pharisees say that Jesus "is not from God, for he does not observe the Sabbath." Michael finally says: "I do not know whether he is a sinner. One thing I do know, that though I was blind, now I see." He and his family are thrown out of their synagogue, and the miracle of healing is lost in the ruckus. But Jesus finds Michael again. He says "Do you believe in the Son of Man?" and Michael responds simply, "Lord, I believe."

What a tale! Michael begins his day begging and ends it seeing for the first time. Behind all the conflict in the story is a clear pool of water, water that brings light to Michael's dark eyes. He's not sure who Jesus is, but at the story's end he kneels to worship Jesus as the Son of Man. Freedom from the law has come to him also, and his eyes are healed. His new life may not be easy, but he has received an extraordinary grace on a Sabbath day.

The Sabbath stories leave us with a feeling of great wonder: Silas stretches out his hand, Delilah stands up straight, Samuel carries his mat, and Michael opens his eyes. We're reminded of a story in Matthew's gospel: from prison, John the Baptist asks Jesus a question through his followers: "Are you the one who is to come, or are we to wait for another?" Jesus answers:

> Go and tell John what you hear and see: the blind receive
> their sight, the lame walk, the lepers are cleansed, the deaf

hear, the dead are raised, and the poor have good news brought to them. (Mt 11: 4–5)

Something new is happening in Israel. And even today, as we struggle with the rules, obligations, and constraints of our own traditions, we can sometimes see that there's a higher way. Often freedom lives in the breaking of bonds. Great grace comes to us at unexpected times.

3

Stories of Foreigners and Outcasts

Besides transformation stories and Sabbath stories, the New Testament holds healing stories of inclusion and acceptance: stories of foreigners and outcasts. If we follow Jesus through the gospels, we see his clear disregard for the forces of wealth, social status, nationality, political party, and law that ostracize those with disease and illness. For him, everyone is accepted. No one lives outside the bounds of Jesus' mercy.

We have already seen Asa, a "foreigner" to the Jews, at Jacob's well. To Jesus, she is an acceptable person. He even eats and sleeps in her city for two days. Yet he is not welcome in his own city, Nazareth, because of his views. In Luke 4:16–30, we hear of Jesus in his home synagogue. He has just returned to Galilee from his baptism and time in the wilderness. Reports begin to spread about him; he teaches in synagogues and receives praise from everyone. But not in Nazareth.

In Nazareth, Jesus goes to the synagogue on the Sabbath and stands to read. He reads from Isaiah 61: "The Spirit of the Lord is upon me, because he has anointed me to bring good news to the poor." He tells the people that the scripture is being fulfilled in their hearing. At first he's spoken well of, but then the rumblings start:

"Is not this Joseph's son?" The conflict begins, with Jesus saying that no prophet is accepted in his own hometown. He then tells two stories, that provoke anger in the listening people.

The first is from 1 Kings 17:1, 8–16, a story of Elijah. Jesus says that in the time of Elijah, when there is terrible famine, the prophet is sent by the Lord to a widow. The widow is to feed and care for him; she lives in Zarephath in Sidon, on the Phoenician coast. "There were many widows in Israel," Jesus says, yet Elijah is sent to a foreigner. He also tells a story from 2 Kings 5:1–14, about Elisha, Elijah's successor. The character in this story is Naaman, "commander of the army of the king of Aram." Naaman is a mighty warrior, but he suffers from leprosy. He finds his way to the Hebrew prophet Elisha, who eventually heals him. "There were also many lepers in Israel," Jesus says, but only Naaman the Syrian is cleansed from his disease.

These two stories infuriate the people in the synagogue at Nazareth: they are a startling rebuff from Jesus for not accepting him as a prophet. The story says the people are "filled with rage." They get up, drive Jesus out of town, and lead him by force to the top of a hill "so that they might hurl him off the cliff." But then an odd thing happens: Jesus "passes through the midst of them and goes on his way." As far as we know, he never goes home again.

What happens here? How does Jesus so narrowly escape death? Do his brothers come to get him, or does he just walk away? We don't know. We know only that Jesus doesn't live in the bounds of traditional Jewish thought. He's living on the borders, on the dangerous fringe, where people outside the camp of Israel are not just unacceptable, but unwelcome. We see here in Jesus a Spirit so large that it can only be feared and misunderstood by those living within safe borders.

Let's now take a look at six stories of outcasts and foreigners: a woman with hemorrhages, a leper, ten more lepers, the calling of Matthew, a Syrophoenician woman, and the centurion's servant. The first four groupings are people in Jesus' own religious tradition; the last two are not Jews. All of them are treated with fear and suspicion by those around them

A Woman with Hemorrhages
(Mt. 9:20–22; Mk. 5:25–34; Lk. 8:43–48)

The woman suffering from hemorrhages appears in all three synoptic gospels. Let's call her Sarah. Her story comes in the middle of the story of Jairus and his daughter. Jesus is on his way to Jairus's house to see his dying daughter, when Sarah gains the courage to move behind him in a crowd of people. She's been suffering from bleeding for twelve years and has "endured much" with several doctors. All her money is gone and she's only grown worse rather than better. She tells herself that if she can just touch the fringe of Jesus' cloak, she'll be made well.

Sarah touches the cloak, and "immediately her hemorrhage stopped." Jesus feels power leave him and turns in the crowd, saying: "Who touched my clothes?" The disciples make a joke of it, as so many people are pressing in. But Jesus remains still, looking around. Sarah then comes "in fear and trembling" and falls down before him, telling him the truth. Jesus calls her daughter, and tells her that her faith has made her well. "Go in peace," he says; "be healed of your disease."

This is a small story within a larger one, but not small in impact. Sarah is ritually unclean according to the laws of Leviticus. Anything she touches is also unclean. But in one moment in a large crowd, Sarah is accepted back into the Jewish community. She is no longer an outcast among her own people. Jesus stops for her: she is cleansed, spoken to, called daughter, and given peace. Jesus seems completely unconcerned that his own clothes are now considered unclean. Sarah must be surprised and amazed: deep peace comes to her, falling like a mantle on her body. She faces Jesus with deep gratitude.

A Leper
(Mt 8:2–4; Mk 1:40–45; Lk 5:12–14)

Other outcasts in Jesus' own religious tradition were lepers. "Leprosy" in Jesus' time and long before referred to a variety of skin diseases, as was the case with Naaman in 2 Kings. In the New

Testament, lepers wind in and out of gospel stories. The leper was also considered unclean, excluded from association with others in the Jewish community. According to Leviticus 13 and 14, a person with leprous disease was to live alone "outside the camp," wear torn clothes and cry out "unclean, unclean." In some cases lepers were to ring a bell, to let people know they were coming. Even after being cured, a leper was not "clean" until ritually purified by a priest.

In all three gospels a leper comes out of nowhere, joining the crowds and following Jesus, who is now teaching, preaching, and healing throughout Galilee. The leper—let's call him David—begs Jesus, kneels down and says: "If you choose, you can make me clean." Jesus is moved with compassion. He stretches out his hand, touches David, and says: "I do choose. Be made clean!" And David is clean. But Jesus leaves him with a stern warning; he tells David to "say nothing to anyone" and further tells him to go to a priest for the ritual purification.

David, in his great excitement, cannot do what Jesus asks. Instead, he tells everyone what the Teacher has done for him. Word spreads fast, and Jesus can no longer go into a town openly. He stays in the country, and people still come to him "from every quarter." We can only assume that David sends every leper he knows to find the Teacher, and we hope that David also goes to see the priest. He is now clean, and acceptable to Jesus, but needs also to be ritually cleansed by the priest. However, David no longer has to ring bells or call out his name: a new peace lives in his heart.

Ten Lepers
(Lk 17:11–19)

In the gospel of Luke, we have another leper story that appears only in this one gospel. This time we have ten lepers, who must live together in a small group outside a village. Jesus is traveling the region between Samaria and Galilee, and the lepers approach him as he nears their village. They keep their distance, shouting and calling out to him: "Jesus, Master, have mercy on us!" Jesus sees them and tells them to show themselves to the priests.

As the lepers go their way, they were made clean. One of the lepers, seeing that he is healed, runs back to Jesus "praising God with a loud voice." He falls at Jesus' feet and thanks him. The story then adds: "And he was a Samaritan." Jesus responds with questions: Weren't ten made clean? Where are the other nine? Then he adds: Is this foreigner the only one to praise God? He tells the Samaritan leper that his faith has made him well, and Luke's point is made. Once again we have an outcast being made whole, and the outcast is a Samaritan. The other lepers, presumably Jews, never turn around after becoming clean. But the Samaritan "prostrated himself at Jesus' feet."

The Calling of Matthew
(Mt 9:9–13; Mk 2:13–17; Lk 5:27–32)

Before going on to stories of other foreigners and Jesus, let's look at one more within Jesus' own tradition: the calling of Matthew. This is not a story of physical healing, but one more example of the acceptance Jesus gave to outcasts, those living outside the camp. Matthew, like Zacchaeus, is a tax collector. In the gospel of Matthew he is called Matthew; for Mark and Luke he is Levi, son of Alphaeus.

The story opens abruptly, with Jesus "walking along." He sees Matthew/Levi sitting at a tax booth and says: "Follow me." Matthew gets up, leaves everything, and follows Jesus. Later we hear of a great banquet at Levi's house, including assorted "tax collectors and sinners" as guests. The Pharisees say to Jesus' disciples: "Why does your teacher eat with tax collectors and sinners?" Jesus overhears and tells them that people who are well don't need a physician. Then he says: "Go and learn what this means, 'I desire mercy, not sacrifice.'" He refers to Hosea 6:6, using scripture to rebut the Pharisees, much to their discomfort. Jesus doesn't consider propriety, tradition, or manners; all are welcome at his table.

In this story we have a moment in Matthew's life when he gets up and follows Jesus. How long has he been sitting at his tax table, collecting money for Rome? Did his father sit there before him? We don't know. We do know he is probably wealthy, probably not well liked, and perhaps tired of sitting and counting coins. Luke makes clear that he not only gets up, but he leaves *everything* behind. For once in his life, someone has wanted his company; Matthew is accepted, and with this acceptance he becomes a new person.

A Syrophoenician Woman
(Mt. 15:21–28; Mk. 7:24–30)

Besides the bleeding woman, the begging lepers, and the tax man counting coins, we have gospel stories of people a Jew would not normally have had contact with: a Syrophoenician woman and her daughter, a Roman centurion and his son. We've already heard the stories of the Samaritan woman at the well, Naaman the Syrian, and the widow of Zarephath—all people outside Judaism. Now we'll look at two stories where Jesus crosses the line between Jews and Gentiles, between those of his own camp and those belonging to other countries and territories.

The Syrophoenician woman appears in the gospels of Matthew and Mark. In Matthew she is called "a Canaanite" from the region of Tyre and Sidon; in Mark she is a "Gentile, of Syrophoenician origin." Jesus is traveling near the Phoenician cities of Tyre and Sidon, far north of Jerusalem. The story begins, "He entered a house and did not want anyone to know he was there." But the woman—let's call her Chloe—comes anyway. She shouts: "Have mercy on me, Lord, Son of David; my daughter is tormented by a demon."

To this outburst Jesus says nothing at all, at least in Matthew. Matthew, known to be the most "Jewish" of all the gospels, has the disciples telling Jesus to "send her away," to which he responds: "I was sent only to the lost sheep of the house of Israel." In both gospels Chloe still comes in humility and bows at Jesus' feet. She says, "Lord, help me," and begs Jesus to take the demon from her daughter.

Jesus responds with a harsh, curt statement: "Let the children be fed first, for it is not fair to take the children's food and throw it to the dogs." Chloe understands that Jesus refers to the Jews as children, and the Gentiles as dogs. But she presses on with her request: yes, she says, but "even the dogs under the table eat the children's crumbs." "Woman, great is your faith!" Jesus exclaims. He grants her request, saying the demon has left her daughter. Chloe goes home to find her daughter lying in bed, restored to health.

In Chloe we have a woman who is put to the test not once, but twice: first by the disciples who are tired of her shouting, and second by Jesus. She is a nonbelieving believer who puts all her faith in the healing power of the Jewish prophet from Galilee. We don't know the original intent of this story—whether to persuade readers of Gentile inclusion or to show prejudice against women and non-Jews—but in the end, the woman's request is granted. How happy Chloe is to find her young daughter well again; no more shouting or trouble at home, just peace and joy.

The Centurion's Servant
(Mt 8:5–13; Lk 7:1–10; Jn 4:46–53)

Our final story of Jesus and a person outside his own tradition is that of the Roman centurion and his slave, or son. In Matthew and Luke the man—let's call him Julius— is a "centurion," a Gentile military officer in command of one hundred soldiers. Julius is concerned for his servant or slave who is paralyzed (Matthew) or ill and close to death (Luke). In Matthew the centurion comes directly to Jesus; in Luke he sends Jewish elders to Jesus, asking for help. They tell Jesus the centurion is worthy, "for he loves our people, and it is he who built our synagogue for us." In Matthew and Luke, the story takes place in Capernaum, by the Sea of Galilee.

In the gospel of John the story takes an interesting turn. Jesus is now in Cana, where he changed water into wine, almost twenty miles away. Julius is now a "royal official," and his son in Caper-naum, is close to death. Julius comes to Jesus and begs for the life of his son: "Sir, come down before my little boy dies." Jesus tells him to go, that his son will live; indeed, the fever leaves the son that very hour, even though it takes the official another day to return home. This miracle transforms the lives of many besides Julius: "So he himself believed, along with his whole household."

Once again details in these stories shift and change, perhaps due to the tellers, or to the years gone by before the stories were written down. But one thing is clear: Jesus listens to someone different from himself—a Roman, and a military officer. In Matthew, when the centurion expresses his bedrock belief in Jesus' authority, Jesus is "amazed" and tells those around him: "Truly I tell you, in no one in Israel have I found such faith." In Luke, before Jesus reaches the man's house, the Roman sends word telling Jesus not to trouble himself, "for I am not worthy to have you come under my roof." He asks Jesus to "only speak the word" that his servant might be healed.

In every telling, Julius is a humble man with a willing heart, unusual qualities for someone in his position. He is not a Jew, but he has helped build a place of worship for the Jews, and now his kindness is being repaid. He and Jesus seem to have respect for one another; Julius even shows respect for his valued slave. This feeling of tolerance and good will permeates the story in all its versions, and in the end, the one in need of healing is healed.

These stories of outcasts and foreigners, so very ancient, speak powerfully to our own day. How often do we think that our way is the only way, that our tradition is the only tradition? We are used to our own kind and our own clan. Others coming in are intruders, or at suspect best. Yet Jesus seems fearless in reaching out to those unlike himself: women with blood disorders, lepers with skin dis-eases, tax collectors and sinners, Gentile women and Roman sol-diers. His tolerance and acceptance shine like a light for the rest of us to follow.

⚜ 4 ⚜

Friends' Stories

The gospels also hold a treasure of stories about friends and healing. Not all of the people healed in the gospels, were healed in isolation. Not all were as courageous in approaching Jesus as the bleeding woman, the leper in the crowd, or the ten lepers outside the village. We have already seen two people—the Syrophoenician woman and the Roman centurion—who speak as intercessors for their family members. But there are many others as well: family members, friends, or relatives who bring to Jesus those who cannot bring themselves. They come in kindness and desperation and love, hoping for a healing touch.

Great Crowds
(Mt 14:35, 36; Mk 6:54–56; Mt 15:30,31) (Mt 4:23–25;
Mk 1:29–34; Mk 3:10; Lk 4:38–40) (Mt 12:15–16; Lk 6:17–19)

All of the gospels relate stories of great crowds gathering around Jesus, wherever he went. Matthew 9:35 tells us that Jesus goes to "all the cities and villages;" he teaches in the synagogues, proclaims good news of the kingdom, and cures every disease and sickness. Mark 3:10 and Matthew 4:24, 25 say that when Jesus leaves with his disciples to go to sea, a great multitude from Galilee follow him. People come in "great numbers" from Judea, Jerusalem, Idumea, beyond the Jordan, and the region of Tyre and Sidon. In Mark's telling, Jesus has his disciples ready a boat because of the crowd, "so that they would not crush him."

In Matthew 14:35, 36 and Mark 6:54–56 people are trying to touch even the fringe of Jesus' cloak. In this scene, Jesus and the disciples land at Gennesaret and moor their boat. People recognize him, send word to others, and begin to "bring the sick on mats to wherever they heard he was." In villages, cities, and farms, family members and friends lay their sick in marketplaces and beg to touch the corners of Jesus' cloak. The fringe—blue twisted threads at the four corners of male garments—acts as a reminder to obey God's commandments. The story says all who touch the fringe are healed. How powerful a scene this is, with scores of people bringing those unable to bring themselves! Kindness, love, and mercy fill these stories.

The faith of the people continues in other scenes: Matthew 15:30, 31 tells of "great crowds" bringing with them "the lame, the maimed, the blind, the mute, and many others." The friends and relatives put all these people at Jesus' feet, and he cures them:

> . . .so that the crowd was amazed when they saw the mute speaking, the maimed whole, the lame walking, and the blind seeing. And they praised the God of Israel.

Two other passages, Mark 1:29–34, and Luke 4:38–40, speak of crowds and healing. Jesus and his companions go to Capernaum in Galilee, where he teaches in the synagogue on the Sabbath. He then enters the house of brothers Simon and Andrew, along with James and John. Simon's mother-in-law is in bed with a fever, and Jesus takes her by the hand and "lifts her up." The fever leaves, and she serves the men their supper. That evening at sundown, the townspeople bring to him all who are sick; as the story says, "the whole city was gathered around the door."

A Paralytic
(Mt 9:1–8; Mk 2:1–12; Lk 5:17–26)

The kindness of friends continues with the story of a paralyzed man, found in the three synoptic gospels. Jesus has returned to Simon's household in Capernaum, and news of this is reported around town. So large are the crowds coming to Jesus that there's no longer room, "not even in front of the door" (Mark). Four people then come carrying a paralyzed man. The crowd is so great that the people remove the roof above Jesus and lower the paralytic man on his mat. Luke tells us: "They went up on the roof and let him down with his bed through the tiles into the middle of the crowd in front of Jesus."

When Jesus sees the faith of the man's friends and family, he turns to the paralytic and says: "Son, your sins are forgiven." The scribes and Pharisees present then ask: "Who is this who is speaking blasphemies? Who can forgive sins but God alone?" Jesus tells the man—let's call him Ezra—to take up his bed and go home. Ezra walks out before the entire crowd, who are amazed. Luke reports that the people glorified God and were filled with awe: "We have seen strange things today." In Mark's version they exclaim, "We have never seen anything like this!"

Ezra's story is rare. Not only is he healed, but his friends and family are so determined to reach Jesus that they tear up Simon's roof. Their kindness is paralleled only by their fortitude: they won't give up until Ezra is placed before the feet of Jesus. The miracle of the healing is almost lost in the anger and debate, but in the end Ezra walks out with his mat, surrounded by people who care.

A Deaf Man *(Mk 7:31–37)* and A Blind Man *(Mk 8:22–26)*

The gospel of Mark contains two other small stories, of a deaf man and a blind man who were also helped by friends and family. In both cases Jesus lays his hands on them, as he does repeatedly in his healing practice. This method, common to healers of his time, also became the practice of the disciples. In Acts 8:17 Peter and John lay their hands on believers; in Acts 9:17 disciple Ananias lays his hands on Saul's blind eyes; in Acts 28:8 Paul lays his hands on a man lying sick in bed.

In these Markan stories we see this practice firsthand, with Jesus. The disciples have been north in the seaside regions of Tyre and Sidon, and now they walk south to Galilee and the Decapolis region, in eastern Palestine. People bring to Jesus a deaf man with a speech impediment, "and they begged him to lay his hand on him." Jesus takes the man aside: he puts his fingers into his ears, spits, and touches his tongue. Then he says: *Ephphatha,* "Be opened." The deaf man's ears are opened, and he begins to speak plainly. The people are "astounded beyond measure." The use of the Aramaic word *ephphatha* here, rather than the Greek, suggests an actual eye-witness account. The other story in the gospel of Mark also has family and friends assisting. This time the disciples are in Bethsaida, a large village above the Sea of Galilee. People bring a blind man to Jesus and "begged him to touch him." Jesus takes the blind man by the hand and leads him out of the village; he puts saliva on his eyes, lays his hands on him, and asks: "Can you see anything?" The man looks up and says: "I can see people, but they look like trees, walking." Jesus places his hands on the man's eyes a second time; this time, the man sees "everything clearly."

These two stories have some things in common: both have friends bringing the suffering person, and both of the men are taken aside, away from the large crowds. Jesus also tells both men to "tell no one;" to keep the healings quiet. Clearly he's concerned about the publicity the healings will cause, but he also shows great kindness to the men, and to their friends and families. Kindness and mercy prevail, as the "kingdom of heaven" comes closer to earth.

Two Blind Men
(Mt 9:27–31; Mt 20:29–34)

In these two stories, both from the gospel of Matthew, no one presents the blind men to Jesus; rather, they help and support each other. Perhaps they've known each other a long time, or perhaps they sit on the same roadside together, begging for coins. In Matthew 9, Jesus is still traveling through the Sea of Galilee region. The two blind men begin to follow him and his company, and they shout for attention: "Have mercy on us, Son of David!"

Jesus leaves the road, enters a house, and the blind men also enter. Let's call them Jacob and James. Jesus turns to the men and asks a question: "Do you believe that I am able to do this?" They answer, "Yes, Lord." Then he touches both pairs of eyes, and their eyes are opened. Jesus tells Jacob and James that this has been done to them according to their faith. He also tells them to make no mention of the healing: "See that no one knows of this." But in their joy, the two friends spread the news.

Jesus extends mercy in another story of two blind men, found in Matthew 20. This story is usually linked with Mark 10:46–52 and Luke 18:35–43, as all three stories take place in Jericho. Jesus and a crowd are leaving Jericho, a main city on a trade route not far from the River Jordan. Two blind men sit by the roadside and hear Jesus as he passes. They shout for mercy; the crowd tells them to be quiet, but they shout even more: "Have mercy on us!" Jesus stops, calls them, and asks what they want. They say, "Lord, let our eyes be opened." The story says Jesus is "moved with compassion," and he touches their eyes.

In Matthew's stories, kindness, compassion, and mercy are all intertwined. The word *compassion* shows up in many gospel stories: with Jesus and a leper (Mk 1:41), the master and the unforgiving debtor (Mt 18:27), the Good Samaritan (Lk 10:33), the prodigal son (Lk 15:20). In our stories of blind men, Jesus stops what he's doing, asks questions, and gives attention. Then in compassion and with great pity he heals their sightless eyes. The men call out for the mercy they need, and mercy comes to them.

Blind Bartimaeus
(Mk 10:46–52; Lk 18:35–43)

Bartimaeus, son of Timaeus, shows up by name only in the gospel of Mark. The Lukan version is similar, with an unnamed man. Both of these stories, like the last one discussed, take place in Jericho. This story is similar to the others, but this time some in the crowd encourage and assist the man. Bartimaeus is sitting by the roadside, in his familiar place, earning a very small living. He hears a crowd and asks: What's happening? Several people tell him Jesus of Nazareth is passing by.

Hearing this, Bartimaeus goes into action and shouts the familiar words: "Son of David, have mercy on me!" Many tell Bartimaeus to stop shouting, but he continues to cry out. Jesus stands still and says: "Call him here." Hostility changes to kindness as some people tell the blind man that Jesus is asking for him. "Take heart," they say; "get up, he is calling you." Bartimaeus throws off his cloak and springs up. Jesus asks him what he wants, and he replies: "My teacher, let me see again."

This story seems different from the others simply because of a few details. "Take heart. . .he is calling you" is one of the most touching phrases in the gospels. Some people, perhaps disciples themselves, decide to encourage Bartimaeus rather than revile him; they show him kindness. Bartimaeus, for his part, is so happy that he throws off his cloak and leaves it behind. He addresses Jesus with a familiar "my rabbi" and regains his sight. Bartimaeus finds healing with a little help from his friends.

The Boy with a Spirit
(Mt 17:14–21; Mk 9:14–29; Lk 9:37–43)

Our word *compassion*, occurs again in a story of a father interceding for his son. This story appears in all three synoptic gospels. The son has a "spirit" or a demon, which makes him "foam and grind his teeth, and become rigid"—what we would now call an epileptic. In this situation, Jesus sees himself as pitted against an unclean spirit. Morton Kelsey remarks:

> Jesus' underlying attitude was that the demon-possessed and the physically ill were under the influence or control of an evil power. Some evil sources—demons, Satan, something destructive and uncreative, the very opposite of the Holy Spirit—seemed to have gained control or at least have a partial influence over the sick person. (71)

In our story, Jesus has come down from the mountain of Transfiguration, along with Peter, James, and John. They join the rest of the disciples, who have around them a large crowd, including scribes. The scribes and disciples are arguing: a man steps forward and tells Jesus he has brought his son, an only child, to be healed. The child, he says, has a spirit that makes him unable to speak, and when it "seizes him, it dashes him down. . ." The father says the disciples cannot cast this spirit out.

Jesus becomes very angry: "You faithless generation, how much longer must I be among you? How much longer must I put up with you? Bring him to me." The boy comes, falls on the ground and rolls around, foaming at the mouth. The father says: "If you are able to do anything, have pity on us, and help us." He asks for compassion. Jesus says that all things can be done for the one who believes. The father then cries out a heartfelt line: "I believe; help my unbelief!"

Here we have compassion operating on both sides. The father is desperate to help his son; let's call them Isaiah and Eli. Eli has been this way since he was quite young, and his condition has broken Isaiah's heart. But Isaiah still champions his son: First he lands in the middle of a conflict between scribes and disciples, with no one helping. Then he risks Jesus' anger and continues to press his case. Isaiah says the demon has thrown his son into fire and water, and he asks, quite simply, for help. He is so worn out after years of these seizures that he'll do anything. I want to believe, he says; help me to believe. In the end, Eli takes Jesus' hand, and he stands up.

These stories of friends and family members are amazing: people carrying loved ones on mats, from village to town to farm, hoping for the Teacher's touch; friends taking apart roofs to lower their loved one at Jesus' feet; people begging Jesus to lay his hands on the deaf, the mute, the lame, the blind. We have blind people shouting to be heard, and a father remaining faithful to his only son. In these stories we can see the great love and great compassion available to us, when we ask for assistance and help. Perhaps when all else fails, our friends and family won't let us down: we'll be cared for, borne to safe places, and healed.

⚜ 5 ⚜

Death Stories

Our Lord's resurrection—unless one is unerringly orthodox—has been explained in a great variety of ways by different strands of believers, over long periods of time. In our own time, John Dominic Crossan, a former Roman Catholic priest and scholar of the Jesus Seminar, believes Jesus' body was disposed of by dogs after the crucifixion, as was the custom of the time. Anglican Bishop John Spong does not believe in a bodily resurrection, ascension, or post-resurrection appearances. One of my esteemed seminary professors believed in a "full-tomb" theory; others believe in the empty tomb and physical resurrection.

Others in the Christian community believe that Jesus never actually died, but that he was drugged and taken down from the cross early due to the approaching Sabbath. And somewhere amongst all these theories are those who believe that the body was actually stolen by disciples while the guards slept—the story the Jews themselves put forward. As one conservative seminary professor said to me: these things are talked about, but only in quiet corners, over quiet lunches.

The New Testament writings, themselves, hold four stories of raisings from the dead. Three are in the gospels, one in the Acts of the Apostles: Talitha daughter of Jarius; the widow's son at Nain; Lazarus in the tomb; and Tabitha, also called Dorcas, with the widows at Joppa. I'll present these stories as they are, from the various texts. Did Jesus and Simon Peter really raise these people from the dead? Were they actually dead, or just in comas? Translating first century writings to twenty-first century understanding is no easy task. But we can understand raisings in our own lives, and we can experience joy. Faith and reason translate the rest. Let's look then at four stories containing every possible emotion, in settings both quiet and dramatic.

Talitha, Daughter of Jairus
(Mt 9:18–26; Mk 5:21–43; Lk 8:40–56)

Talitha's story frames that of the woman with the hemorrhage. Jesus and his followers are again in the area of Capernaum, which seems now to be his "own town" (Mt. 9:1), on the sea of Galilee. A leader of the local synagogue named Jairus comes to Jesus, when Jesus and a great crowd are gathered by the sea. Jairus falls at Jesus' feet and repeatedly begs: "My little daughter is at the point of death." He asks Jesus to lay hands on her, so she might live. Talitha is Jairus's only daughter, twelve years old. Jesus agrees to go to her.

At this point the story of the bleeding woman intervenes. When we catch up with Jairus again, someone from his household has come to say his daughter is dead, and thus tells him not to trouble the Teacher. Jesus says to Jairus: "Do not fear, only believe." Peter, James, and John go with Jesus and Jairus the rest of the way to his house. A crowd with flute players and mourners is gathered; the people are loudly "weeping and wailing." Jesus tells them: "The child is not dead but sleeping." The people laugh at him.

In the story's next scene, Jesus, the father, the mother, Peter, James, and John go into the daughter's room; all other people are put outside. We don't see a picture of the little girl, but Jesus takes her by the hand and says *"Talitha cum,"* telling her to get up. In another version he says "Child, get up!" Talitha begins to walk around, and the parents are "overcome with amazement." Jesus tells them to keep the incident quiet, and he also tells the family to give their daughter something to eat.

This wonderful gospel story again retains the original Aramaic words, *Talitha cum,* suggesting eyewitnesses to the incident. We don't know the end of this story for Talitha and her family, but we do feel the gamut of emotion: weeping, begging, fear, dread, despair, small hope, amazement, and great joy. Talitha's father and mother are beyond joy that their small child, seemingly dead, is now alive. As for the child herself, we don't actually see her or hear her in the story, but she's very much alive: Talitha wakes, she walks, she eats, she holds the hand of the Teacher who has just given back her life. She feels a deep joy.

Widow's Son at Nain
(Lk 7:11–17)

The writer of the gospel of Luke also records a raising story, "the widow's son at Nain." Luke is partial to women and widows throughout his gospel. In this story neither son nor mother is named. Jesus, his disciples, and a large crowd have just arrived at Nain, to the southwest of Capernaum. As they approach the town's gate, a man who has died is being carried out on a bier, to be buried outside the city walls. He is "his mother's only son," and she is a "widow." A crowd has come out from the town to comfort the mother. Jesus sees the woman, feels compassion for her, and speaks to her. "Do not weep," he says.

Then Jesus comes to the funeral procession and touches the dead man's bier. The bearers stand still. Jesus says: "Young man, I say to you, rise!" The dead man sits up and speaks, and Jesus gives him to his mother. Fear seizes all the people, who glorify God and say: "A great prophet has risen among us!" Because of this extraordinary happening, word of Jesus and his touch spreads throughout Judea and the surrounding countryside.

We don't know where this small story comes from. It doesn't appear in any of the gospels besides Luke. But two stories of women, sons, and raisings do appear in ancient Hebrew texts: Elijah and the widow of Zarephath (1 Kings 17:17–24) and one with Elisha and the Shunammite woman (2 Kings 4: 25–37). In both stories, sons of the women are "raised from the dead" or restored to life with much effort by the prophets. But here, in Luke's story, all Jesus does is touch the bier and call to the young man. He rises, and returns to life.

Emotions run high in this very small story. Once again we are told of Jesus' *compassion* for someone in distress. The widow has suddenly found herself without financial support, very much alone. Her grief is deep, but in an unexpected moment, the grief turns to fear and then to joy. "God has looked favorably on his people!" her friends shout, and the son lives again. Even on the bier, in the stillness of death, the young man has felt the Teacher's healing touch.

The Raising of Lazarus
(Jn 11:1–57)

The story of the raising of Lazarus has been as well-known for centuries as the stories of the resurrection itself. Lazarus is brother to

Mary and Martha of Bethany, and the family is close to Jesus. Bethany is a small village near Jerusalem, and the sisters welcome Jesus to their home (Lk 10:38–42). In the long story of John 11, Lazarus falls ill. The sisters send a message to Jesus, in the north country: "Lord, he whom you love is ill." Jesus seems unconcerned. He says that the illness doesn't lead to death, and it is "for God's glory."

Jesus stays where he is two days longer, although the story confirms that he loves Martha, Mary, and Lazarus. Then he tells his disciples to prepare for a trip to Judea. The disciples are unhappy: "Rabbi, the Jews were just now trying to stone you, and are you going there again?" Jesus answers cryptically, asking: "are there not twelve hours of daylight?" Then he tells them: "Our friend Lazarus has fallen asleep, but I am going there to awaken him." Disciple Thomas says: Let us also go, to die with him. They begin the long walk, but by the time they arrive, Lazarus has already been four days in the tomb.

Martha hears Jesus is on his way and travels out to meet him. She says: "Lord, if you had been here, my brother would not have died." Jesus tells her that Lazarus will rise again, and they speak of resurrection, with Martha confessing faith. Jesus asks for Mary, and she and other Jews join the scene. By now, everyone is weeping, including Jesus. The Jews say: "See how he loved him!" Jesus, "greatly disturbed in spirit and deeply moved," goes to Lazarus's tomb, a cave with a stone lying against it. He stops and says: "Take away the stone."

Martha protests. She tells Jesus there will be "a stench" after so many days. Jesus tells her she will see the glory of God, and he has the stone removed. Then he says a prayer and calls with a loud voice: "Lazarus, come out!" The dead man walks out, his hands, feet, and face bound with strips of cloth. Jesus says: "Unbind him, and let him go." And from this time on, the chief priests and Pharisees plan to put Jesus to death. Jesus no longer goes openly among the people, but instead leaves for the wilderness.

Emotions run high in this powerful story, especially the joy of those present at the raising. But the story is interrupted by the political situation—with Caiaphas the high priest and the Jewish Sanhedrin council—so that we never see what happens after Lazarus is unbound. What does he say? Where does he go? Who believes in this astounding event? We hear later on, when Martha holds a dinner party for Jesus, that Lazarus is also present at table. A crowd comes to see him, and the chief priests plan "to put Lazarus to death as well," since many Jews now believe in Jesus. His raising of Lazarus to life is the beginning of Jesus' death.

Tabitha the Gazelle
(Acts 9:36–43)

We make a very big time leap now, to the story of Tabitha, also called Dorcas, written in the Acts of the Apostles. Acts takes place after Jesus' crucifixion and resurrection, when the Way, the new Christian community, begins to form. This story shows the work and tradition of Jesus being carried on by the first generation of followers. This time the one doing the raising from the dead is Simon Peter, who has traveled with Jesus and shared his home in Capernaum. Peter's life is no longer what it used to be when he was a simple fisherman; now he takes up Jesus' traveling ministry, going "here and there among all the believers" (9:32).

As a preface to our story, Peter is with "the saints living in Lydda," a large city to the north and west of Jerusalem—where Peter and others remained after Jesus' death. Lydda is in the plain of Sharon, ten miles southeast of Joppa by the sea. In Lydda, Peter comes upon a man called Aeneas, who has been bedridden and paralyzed for eight years. Peter tells him: "Aeneas, Jesus Christ heals you; get up and make your bed!" Aeneas gets up, and more become believers.

After this, we are introduced to Tabitha (Aramaic) or Dorcas (Greek); both of her names mean *gazelle*. Tabitha lives in Joppa, and she's a disciple "devoted to good works and acts of charity." But she becomes ill and dies. Tabitha is washed by friends, according to custom, and her body is laid in an upstairs room. Disciples hear that Peter is in Lydda, and they send two men, asking him to "come to us without delay." Peter travels from Lydda up to Joppa with the men and is taken to Tabitha's upstairs room.

At the house, Peter finds many widows gathered, who weep,

showing him tunics and clothing that Tabitha has made for them. He puts all the women outside, then goes to Tabitha, where he kneels and prays. He turns to the body and says: "Tabitha, get up." The dead woman opens her eyes and sits up. Peter gives her his hand, then calls all the "saints and widows," showing Tabitha to be alive. Many believe in this great miracle, and joy abounds in the upper room.

Tabitha's story is the only New Testament instance where the feminine form of the word *disciple* is used. She's also the only New Testament person to be raised from the dead by a disciple of Jesus. Her story relates to the belief within the Way that Jesus would soon return, and that when he did, he would take the saints and believers with him—to a new heaven and a new earth. Thus the great anxiety on the part of the faithful at Joppa; they want Tabitha alive and well for the second coming of the Lord. Imagine their feelings of thankfulness!

All of these stories of miraculous raisings—Jairus and his little daughter Talitha, the widow and her son on the funeral bier, Lazarus and his sisters Mary and Martha, Tabitha and the widows of Joppa—hold immense power, whether viewed as literal raisings going beyond medical explanation or as raisings symbolizing the light and life of Jesus. They contain every human emotion and end with astounding joy. Talitha takes Jesus' hand, the son sits up on the bier, Lazarus walks out from the tomb, and Tabitha opens her eyes. The joy in these stories surpasses any questions we might have of how they actually happened.

Even in our darkest moments, we can recall one or more of these stories and remember how they have been passed down with love and devotion, through centuries and generations. Jesus touches the child and touches the son's bier, bringing life to both. Lazarus's bandages come unraveled, and he's freed from the darkness of the tomb. Tabitha sees all the people she loves once again and rejoins her community of faith. Our daily deaths and sufferings do not have final power over us. Raisings happen, again and again. As the psalmist says: "Weeping may linger for the night, but joy comes with the morning" (30:5).

We have now looked at a number of biblical healing stories: *transformation stories* having to do with deep forgiveness; *Sabbath stories* having to do with freedom and the breaking of bonds; *stories of foreigners and outcasts,* having to do with inclusion and acceptance outside the norm of the tribe; *friends' stories,* showing love, mercy, and kindness; and *death stories,* with an abundance of fear, sadness, and joy. If you've never read these stories, or if you're reading them anew, it's my hope that you'll find here what you need to find: a word of comfort, a touch of peace, a sense that others before have longed for the same things. There is much to be revisited in these beautiful stories.

And there is more to consider, much more, including the *deep peace* these stories bring. For that's what it all comes down to—that River running beneath all the emotions and varying scenes of life. Our Lord was no stranger to that peace, despite his constant situations of conflict. He knew this peace so well that part of our ancient eucharistic liturgy includes "the Peace"—when we say *"Peace of the Lord"* to one another. In Jesus was this peace, and it remained long after he was gone, causing fearful people to find courage, downtrodden people to find hope, and unbelieving people to find their faith.

How do we use these stories now? Perhaps there's one that moves you and relates to your present situation, or perhaps one that amazes you and helps you to see more clearly. Or even one that brings you to your knees, to ask for the help. Good stories do this very thing: they hold up a long and shining mirror, so that we see not only characters in stories but ourselves in a clear light. We understand ourselves better, and thus we know more peace.

The healing stories, then, bring us to a place we never left, to the River running deep in our lives. John's gospel leaves us with these enduring words of Jesus:

> Peace I leave with you; my peace I give to you. I do not give to you as the world gives. Do not let your hearts be troubled, and do not let them be afraid. (Jn 14:27)

Most of the time, we are lost in the past or carried away by the future. When we are mindful, deeply in touch with the present moment, our understanding of what is going on deepens, and we begin to be filled with acceptance, joy, peace, and love.
—Thich Nhat Hanh, *The Long Road Turns to Joy*

II. HEALING PRAYER

Thich Nhat Hanh, a Buddhist monk and Zen master, is one of the greatest peacemakers of our time. What he's talking about in this quotation—being filled with acceptance, joy, peace, and love—is something that takes a good while. In my first year with Shalem Institute, we sat on the floor in a long-term group, once weekly for several months, experiencing deep silence. During this time my mind loved to chatter, to amuse itself by throwing up on the screen nice video pictures, nice meditation images to take me far and wide. "Trance and travel" my mentor called it. I would become fascinated, and think I was really getting somewhere, but in truth I was only going farther away from silence. I traveled these avenues for a year before my mind got quiet.

In this part, we'll be talking about ways to find quiet. "Healing Prayer" will be different from "Healing Stories." We'll be leaving behind the wonderful biblical stories for a totally *other* place. This is the place of prayer, known throughout the centuries. And not just prayer, but contemplative prayer. During my first round in seminary, when I wrote a thesis on prayer, I learned about two main categories: *active* and *contemplative prayer*. The first has to do with talking to or praising God. There are five kinds of active prayer: adoration, thanksgiving, confession, petition, intercession. Every morning in chapel I knelt down to begin my prayers.

I continued this active prayer for several years following seminary, but slowly I found myself wearing out, or actually wearing down to a deeper kind of prayer. I was moving into silence. This kind of silence has been practiced for centuries by holy zealots in the desert, by nuns and monks in convents and monasteries, and by ordinary people like you and me. George Garrett, in his poem *Buzzard*, speaks of this prayer in silence as "holy madness":

> I've heard that holy madness is a state
> not to be trifled with, not to be taken
> lightly by jest or vow, by lover's token
> or any green wreath for a public place. Flash
> in the eyes of madmen precious fountains,
> whose flesh is wholly thirst, insatiate.
>
> I see this bird with grace begin to wheel,
> glide in God's fingerprint, a whorl
> of night, in light a thing burnt black,
> unhurried. Somewhere something on its back
> has caught its eye. Wide-winged he descends,
> like angels, to the business of this world.
>
> I've heard that saintly hermits, frail, obscene
> in rags, slack-fleshed, with eyes like jewels, kneel
> in dry sand, among the tortured mountains, feel
> at last the torment of their prayers take shape,
> take wings, assume the brutal rush of grace.
> This bird comes then and picks those thin bones clean.

Perhaps contemplative prayer is like jewels in the eyes of hermits, bringing us to clearer silence and deeper peace. "Healing Prayer will consider several kinds of contemplative prayer used throughout the centuries. First, we'll consider briefly the prayer of

Jesus: his customs, practice, and teachings. Then we'll go on to other types of meditative prayer, both nontraditional and traditional: *Open Prayer, Word Prayer,* and *Visual Prayer.* Within these, we'll look at a variety of prayers, such as breathing and centering, Jesus Prayer and Mary Prayer, icon and symbol meditation. Each of these is a small jewel of its own: prayers that "take shape, take wings" through practice and time.

✢ 1 ✢

The Prayer of Jesus

Jesus' Prayers and Customs

We know of only one prayer that Jesus actually taught his disciples, the *Lord's Prayer* (Mt 6:9–13, Lk 11:2–4). This was not a contemplative prayer, but an end-time or eschatological prayer, serving practical purposes for people expecting a new kingdom: "give us each day our daily bread," as they were hungry; "forgive us our sins, for we ourselves forgive everyone indebted to us," as they wished to be without sin; "your kingdom come," as this was their hope. The disciples ask Jesus to teach them to pray outside synagogue tradition, and this is what he teaches them.

The recorded prayers of Jesus are very few and sometimes brief. There is a *prayer of thanksgiving* (Mt 11:25, 26; Lk 10:21, 22) when Jesus gives thanks for his followers; a *prayer of petition* (Mt 26:39; Mk 14:36; Lk 22:42) when he asks not to die; a *prayer of intercession* (Lk 23:34) for those who have crucified him; a *cry of despair* (Mt 27:46; Mk 15:34) when he feels forsaken; and a *cry of death* (Lk 23:46) when he dies. The fourth gospel adds a few more: *the prayer of thanksgiving* (Jn 11:41, 42) before the raising of Lazarus; the *prayer of obedience* (Jn 12:27, 28) when Jesus' soul is troubled; and the *high priestly prayer* (Jn 17) before his arrest.

Outside these brief instances of Jesus addressing God, we know of no other gospel prayers. We do know there was a regular practice of prayer in the Jewish synagogues, which Jesus most likely kept. The day began with prayers at dawn and ended with prayers at dusk. There was also afternoon prayer at 3 PM, when daily sacrifice was offered in the Temple. In addition, prayers of thanksgiving were said before and after meals. Jesus' own custom was to bless and break bread (Mt 14:19; Mt 15:36; Mt 26:26; Mk 6:41; Mk 8:6; Mk 14:22; Lk 9:16; Lk 22:19; Lk 24:30). Also, every year Jesus' parents "went to Jerusalem" for Passover (Lk 2:41), and he went to the synagogue on the Sabbath day (Lk 4:16).

Jesus' Practice

But it is Jesus' private prayer that carries weight in scripture, although what he actually prays in silence is not known to us. We do know he spends long hours and whole nights in solitary prayer. Mark 1:35 tells us: "In the morning, while it was still very dark, he got up and went out to a deserted place, and there he prayed." He goes to mountains to pray (Mt 14:23; Mk 6:46), he goes to the wilderness to pray (Lk 5:16). Luke 6:12 tells us he spends "the night in prayer to God."

This deep silence gives Jesus his healing power. Without it, he could not face the multitudes of people coming for help. Before the story of the feeding of the five thousand, for instance, the disciples and Jesus are together. The story tells us:

> He said to them, "Come away to a deserted place all by yourselves and rest a while." For many were coming and going, and they had no leisure even to eat. And they went away in the boat to a deserted place by themselves. (Mk 6:31, 32)

When they return, thousands have gathered, who have "hurried there on foot from all the towns." Jesus teaches them many things, and they are miraculously fed. But when evening comes:

> Immediately he made his disciples get into the boat and go on ahead to the other side, to Bethsaida, while he dismissed

the crowd. After saying farewell to them, he went up on the mountain to pray. (Mk 6:45, 46)

In the story of the Transfiguration, Jesus goes to a mountain to pray, taking with him Peter, John, and James (Lk 9:28). Luke tells us: "And while he was praying, the appearance of his face changed, and his clothes became dazzling white" (9:29). Matthew says: "And he was transfigured before them, and his face shone like the sun, and his clothes became dazzling white" (17:2). Mark tells us: ". . .and his clothes became dazzling white, such as no one on earth could bleach them" (9:3). Jesus' prayer fills him with light, so intense is his silence.

Jesus' Teaching

In addition to Jesus' customs and private practice, the New Testament gives us several of his teachings concerning prayer and the spiritual life. Jesus advises us to *ask* for what we want (Mt 7:7–11; Lk 11:9–13), to *seek the kingdom of God* (Mt 6:33; Lk 12:31), and to *have certainty* in prayer (Mk 11:23, 24). Jesus also says to *pray in secret* (Mt 6:6), to *avoid pretense* (Mt 6:7, Mk 12:38–40), and to *forgive*, being reconciled to others, and "forgiving your brother or your sister from your heart" (Mt 18:35; Mt 6:14; Mt 5:23, 24; Mt 5:44; Mk 11:25; Lk 6:28).

Jesus asks his listeners to *watch for the coming kingdom* (Mt 26:41; Mk 13:33; Mk 14:38; Lk 21:36; Lk 22:40) and to *pray for strength*. He tells his disciples to *pray*, in order to heal (Mk 9:29). He tells people to *pray in agreement* (Mt 18: 19, 20), in his name. And last, Jesus says to pray for the kingdom to come, for food, for forgiveness, for strength against evil. The fourth gospel also adds a few passages: *asking in Jesus' name* (Jn 14:13,14; Jn 15:16), and *abiding in Jesus* (Jn 15:4–7, also 6:56; 10:38; 14:10, 11; 15:10), as vines and branches, growing together in an indwelling communion of believers.

This is a very brief summary of what we know concerning Jesus' customs, practice, and teaching. What stand out in all these examples are his own practice of silence and the depth of his prayer; his steadfast trust that God will provide, whatever the circumstances; his strong belief in forgiveness and reconciliation; and his expectant watch for the approaching kingdom. His deep silence in the night gives him the strength to heal, to teach, and to preach, in the new kingdom of heaven on earth.

2

Open Prayer

Now we come to the practice of contemplative prayer. My discussion will offer a "smorgasbord" of things to try, including *open prayer*, *word prayer*, and *visual prayer*. You may find a liking for some of these and not others, but give them all a try. You may wish to practice by yourself, in a small group, or with the assistance of a spiritual director, someone already familiar with various kinds of contemplative prayer. The most important thing is just to begin.

The Dalai Lama, spiritual leader of Tibetan Buddhists, says in his preface to *The Complete Guide to Buddhist America:*

> If we read stories of the great meditative adepts of the past, we find that those who attained high realizations always stayed in peaceful isolated places. There are not many accounts of people who attained great realization in the city or town. Therefore, those who wish to meditate are traditionally advised to cast off attachment to worldly pleasures and comforts and to stay in an isolated place in the forest. (Foreward)

As we've just seen, this is what Jesus did before he went out to the crowds. While most of us are not able to live in a forest, we can at least find a certain place and a certain time to begin practicing silence. Twenty minutes a day in a favorite quiet place is a good start. We can learn little bits of silence daily to carry back to our work, our families, and our world. Let's begin with *breathing meditation,* then go on to *centering prayer, walking, chanting,* and *light.*

Breathing

Breathing is the simplest of meditations, yet also one needing practice. Before sitting, try a few easy body stretches or meditation exercises to help you relax. Then find a comfortable position, either in a straight chair or sitting on floor pillows stacked for elevation so your legs and feet won't go to sleep. Be sure to keep your back straight; imagine a plumb line going down through the center of your body. Relax your belly. Then begin to breathe—slowly and deeply—from the bottom of your belly, up to your lungs. When you breathe in, inhaling deeply, think: *breathing in.* When you breathe out, exhaling deeply, think: *breathing out.* Breathe in, breathe out: relax.

You'll have distractions during the breathing: body aches as well as distractions of noise, vision, time, mind. Your mind will entertain itself with interesting thoughts, or thoughts like *hmmm! maybe now I'm getting somewhere.* Just let these thoughts come, and let them go. A small lighted candle on the floor in front of you may help you keep focus. It also helps to know that thoughts are transitory. As Dom Thomas Keating says, in *Intimacy with God:*

> If we can just rest on a regular basis for twenty to thirty minutes without thinking, we begin to see that we are not our thoughts. We *have* thoughts, but we are not our thoughts. Most people suffer because they think that they are their thoughts and if their thoughts are upsetting, distressing, or evil, they are stuck with them. If they just stopped thinking for awhile every day as a discipline, they would begin to see that they do not have to be dominated by their thoughts. (69)

Counting can also help your breathing. When you inhale and exhale, count *one* in your mind. Then inhale, exhale, count *two,* letting other thoughts and images go. Count in this way, using cycles of inhale and exhale, up to ten; then count backward down to one.

The counting itself is not important, and if you find yourself forgetting numbers, as silence deepens, then just let them go. They may even disappear. The numbers are simply a way into deeper silence, a way of moving to the side the ever-present thoughts.

Lines from psalms can also be used with breathing. One of my favorites is: *"Create in me"* (breathe in), *"a clean heart, O God"* (breathe out). During this breathing you can place your hand over your heart, or visualize your heart being cleansed of all worries/fears/anxieties/thoughts. Again, the words are just a method for taking you down to the River, but familiar parts of psalms are especially comforting: *"The Lord is my shepherd"* (breathe in), *"I shall not want"* (breathe out).

One more word on distracting thoughts: These will not go away any time soon, and you will find yourself mostly in future thoughts (worry) or in past thoughts (regret). It's our nature to suffer this way, living in the future and past. Try to stay in present awareness though, as much as you can. Instead of following the chain of your anxious thoughts: *worry, worry/fear, fear/hope, hope,* let yourself become immersed in what's around you: *chair, tree, sky, candle, light.* When I meditate, I use pillows on the floor, a candle, a meditation bell, and the blue pines outside the window. The pine trees keep me in present time.

When we gain a small amount of present time, we can also let go. Buddhist nun Ayya Khema says, in *Being Nobody, Going Nowhere:*

> To start with, dropping thoughts will only be possible momentarily, but it is a step in the right direction. The spiritual path is all about letting go. There is nothing to achieve or gain. Although these words are used frequently, they are only ways of expressing ourselves. In reality a spiritual path is a path of renunciation, letting go, constantly dropping all we have built up around ourselves. This includes possessions, conditioned habits, ideas, beliefs, thinking patterns. (4)

Breathing is the first step in finding present time and letting go. It's not always an easy practice, as we're not used to slowing down, but once we do, then we can use this practice in small pieces throughout the day. Soon the small pieces will connect together in calm and simple breathing.

Centering Prayer

Centering prayer, like breathing, is an "open" kind of prayer. There are no strings of words to say, nothing to memorize, nothing to think about. You have no place to go, nothing to do, just open space. The more we practice these prayers, the more we realize how much *space* we have in our minds: room for clouds, room for castles, room for the sky; for mountains, forests, rivers, and oceans. We forget that it's been there all along, waiting for us to find it again.

My first experience with centering prayer was at Shalem Institute, while I was a seminarian. I attended a class in the Catholic University area called "Structures of Spirituality." Instead of heavy lectures, the format I was used to, we actually practiced and experienced prayer together as a group. We were told that Thomas Keating and Basil Pennington, Trappist monks, began centering prayer. Zen Buddhist and Christian practice and the writings of Thomas Merton had influenced both men.

The process of centering prayer is very simple: (1) relax into silence, with an opening prayer, then *choose a sacred word* of one or two syllables—or let one rise on its own in the first five minutes; (2) after the word appears, *introduce the sacred word* into your silence as "the symbol of your consent to God's presence;" (3) when you begin to be distracted, simply *return to the word*, using it as a resting place; (4) at the end of your prayer period, *allow a few minutes of silence* before "coming back." Keating recommends twenty to thirty minutes as a minimum time to establish inner silence and get beyond superficial thoughts (*Open,* 37).

Keating says the sacred word is not a "mantra," something to be said repeatedly. The word may even disappear as silence deepens; it's used as a way down, an entry to the river flowing beneath. Our normal thoughts are like many boats crowded on a river, and the sacred word is used to slow down the boats, to allow space between the thoughts. Keating suggests some sacred words: *Lord, Jesus, Abba,*

Father, Mother, Love, Peace, Shalom, Silence (*Open,* 139). My own words have tended to be less traditional, simply what come to me at the time: *home, roses,* the sound of *"ah."* Perhaps the long vowel sounds are helpful in the silence.

Whatever your sacred word, try to let it come on its own, rather than introducing it or forcing it. There may be something buried deep that will pop out and surprise you, if you give it time. Keating recommends not changing your word during prayer periods, as to do this is to "start thinking again." But I have found in leading groups that words often change on their own; sometimes it's best to let them move around until they come to rest on one. You'll soon find your own way! Keating says to practice this prayer twice daily, in the morning and evening.

One word of caution: as there's so much open space in this meditation, the space might cause you to be anxious or unsettled. Keating writes: "Some people, when they are quiet, feel themselves on the edge of a cliff. But don't worry. There is no danger of falling" (*Open,* 42). This fear is natural, as we're not at all used to open space and silence. If you begin to feel anxious, simply put a border around your space. Imagine a clear window that holds your silence and your word; the window has solid borders, to keep you in and keep you safe.

In *Open Mind, Open Heart,* Keating also has two chapters on thoughts, "The Ordinary Kinds of Thoughts" and "The More Subtle Kinds of Thoughts." He tells us to just "start over," when bombarded with distracting thoughts, even good thoughts.

> When we experience the presence of God, if we can just not *think* about it, we can rest in it a long time. Unfortunately, we are like starving people when it comes to spiritual things, and we hang on to spiritual consolation for dear life. It is precisely that possessive attitude that prevents us from enjoying the simplicity and childlike delight of the experience. (85)

Centering prayer is an easy prayer to practice, and you'll find your word becoming an old friend. You can use it in times of prayer, times of stress, times of needing to focus on the stillness within. Some people use their word for several years; others let the word change as time passes by. Either way, your word will become central to your awareness and help you live in present time.

Walking Meditation

Walking meditation is a true joy. It's a type of prayer, but of a different kind altogether. When you do slow walk, you'll feel as if you're swimming in space, and everything will begin to roll past and slow down. Says Thich Nhat Hanh, in *A Guide to Walking Meditation*:

> Walking meditation is practicing meditation while walking. It can bring you joy and peace while you practice it. Take short steps in complete relaxation; go slowly with a smile on your lips, with your heart open to an experience of peace. You can feel truly at ease with yourself. Your steps can be those of the healthiest, most secure person on earth. ("You Can Do It")

Walking meditation is wonderful to do with a group of people or by yourself. When you do walking meditation, you have no purpose other than the walking itself. No place to go, nothing to do: *just walk.* The walk is an intentional slowing down—*heel, toe, breathe; heel, toe, breathe.* You can walk in a circle or straight line, at home, through a green park, past a field of flowers, along a river, or on a beautiful beach. Nhat Hanh says to "place your foot on the surface of the earth the way an emperor would place his seal on a royal decree" ("The Seal of an Emperor").

There is a certain rhythm to the walking. At first you may lose balance, and there will be awkward movements, a feeling of self-consciousness. But if you simply pay attention to your breathing and your slow-moving, rolling steps, you'll soon find a quiet balance. You'll feel like a fish, swimming through the air.

Walking meditation is a harmony of several things: *breathing, counting, half-smile, steps.*

Breathing. We don't usually pay attention to our breathing. We take short, shallow breaths, in between talking and thinking. But in walking meditation, you should take long, deep breaths. Breathe from the bottom of the stomach up, each nice, big breath filling the lungs, expanding them to include air from the sky and sunlight. Breathe slowly and fill your lungs, then exhale, removing all the air. Exhale to the bottom, then just a little bit more. In this way, you'll pay attention to your breathing rather than to the thoughts running like cats and dogs in your mind.

Counting. Counting in combination with your breathing, is also beneficial. You can begin by noticing how many steps you take while breathing in, how many steps you take breathing out. Count them quietly to yourself: *one, two, three; one, two, three.* If your breaths are shallow at first, you may just count *one, two.* The exhalation may also be longer than the inhalation when you begin. Soon you'll have a pattern for breathing and counting (2–2, 2–3, 3–3), and this will change and adjust. The counting itself is not important; it just helps to keep focus.

Half-smile. As you begin your rhythm of breathing and counting, you should also let go of worry and sorrow, fear and anxiety, all the things blocking your way to freedom. This is the time for a smile, the half-smile of peaceful practice. Nhat Hanh says: "Your half-smile and your peaceful steps are bright and shining pearls" ("The String of Pearls"). When you feel yourself frowning, or concentrating on thinking, or walking fast, return to your half-smile. This will help both your posture and your thinking, and it will help others as well. "It not only brings you peace and joy; it also brings peace and joy to people around you" ("Smile Like a Buddha").

Steps. All these processes work together: breathing, counting, smiling, taking your steps. You have no place to go, nothing to do. First find your balance, letting your arms assist the balance and rhythm; let them hang loosely or hold them gently up. Once you find this harmony, then you can notice your steps. Your steps can be calm and courageous. They will become more confident as you drop the baggage weighing you down. "In order to have peace and joy, you must succeed in having peace within each of your steps" ("Your Steps Are Most Important").

Thich Nhat Hanh mentions one more issue in *A Guide to Walking Meditation:* not everyone can walk. During the Vietnam War, many Buddhists lost an arm or a leg, so that they cannot join palms together in greeting, sit in a lotus position, or practice walking meditation. But at Nhat Hanh's home in Plum Village, France, these people sit in chairs and watch others make peaceful steps on the wooden floor. He writes of these monks: "They could make lotus flowers bloom from their footsteps, though they could not walk" ("Let Me Walk With Your Feet"). When we practice our meditation walking, we're walking not just for ourselves, but for the world.

Chanting

I loved singing growing up, and I loved plainsong. Plainsong, or Gregorian chant, comes from very early centuries in the church and was preserved by monasteries and convents through the ages. It's a haunting, sometimes dissonant, minor sound—the music of the old Latin Rite—and it carries with it a great calm. I also remember hearing the beautiful chants of Taizé, the Christian community in France and place of pilgrimage for many thousands. One of Taizé's beloved chants is *"Jesus, Remember Me":*

Jesus, remember me
Jesus, remember me
Jesus, remember me
When you come into your kingdom.

Chanting can take us down to a very quiet place. Sound is powerful, especially if intoned slowly; it blocks out our thoughts and allows for silence among the notes and lines. In prayer groups people have often told me they do not always remember a particular meditation, but they always remember the sound of the bell.

The bell takes them down a long tunnel to a place of rest. Chanting for periods of time creates the same kind of rest and peace. Following are a few examples of chants.

Om/ah/hum. Om—ah—hum is a series of sounds, rather than "thinking" words. Each of these sounds is chanted on the same tone for five to ten seconds. Then the second is chanted, and the third. The sounds dovetail into one another, creating a long, continuous sound. As the "words" have no meaning, no thought is necessary to sustain them: you can just experience the long sounds, chanted anywhere from fifteen minutes to an hour, as well as the silence following once the chant ceases. The joy of doing this with a group of people is hearing the overtones produced; the beautiful higher and lower notes, moving above and below the main sound.

Ubi Caritas. Another beautiful Taizé chant, known to many, is sung in Latin and slowly repeated:

> U-bi car-i-tas, et a-mor
> U-bi car-i-tas, de-us i-bi est.

"Where there is charity, and love; where there is charity, there is God." The effect of this beautiful, simple chant can't be reproduced in these pages, but ask around and you'll hear it; *Ubi Caritas* has been passed from person to person for years. As someone once said to me, the beauty of chanting in another language is that you don't have to pay attention to the words. Instead, the sounds find their way to your heart and mind, letting all other thoughts slip by.

Alleluias and kyries. Other chants are used during the liturgical seasons: *alleluia*s from Easter to Pentecost, and *kyrie*s during Lent or Advent. *Kyrie eleison* (Greek for "Lord, have mercy") can be chanted responsively, with leader and group: *kyr-i-e* (leader) *kyr-i-e* (group); *kyr-i-e e-lei-son* (leader) *kyr-i-e e-lei-son* (group). *Kyrie*s can also be sung together, using the plainsong *kyrie eleison* on page 584 of the 1982 Anglican hymnal. This one in particular may be somewhat difficult at first, but if you have a group leader who knows the sounds, all the other voices will soon fall in place. *Alleluia* chants are the same: sometimes antiphonal, sometimes in unison.

Try experimenting with different kinds and sounds of chants, to see what brings you a sense of deeper peace. The purpose of chant is not to compete with others in a group, but to harmonize voices so no one voice is heard above another. When I lead chant groups, I tell everyone to listen for the voice on either side, then to listen to the group as a whole. In this way no one dominates, and a deeper quiet comes. Thirty minutes total of chanting and silence will work well for a beginning group.

Remember! It's not the words that are important, or even the sounds. What's important is the silence following the sound, leading you down to a quiet river of peace.

Light

The New Testament tells us Jesus taught that God is light: "This is the message we have heard from him and proclaim to you, that God is light and in him there is no darkness at all" (1 Jn 1:5). The "blessing of light" was also a ritual for the Jews at the evening meal. Marion J. Hatchett, in his *Commentary on the American Prayer Book*, tells us that Christians followed this custom at the dinner table, as the oldest of evening services:

> Evidence of such Christian ritual appears in the Apostolic Tradition of Hippolytus (Rome, c. A.D. 215). The evening service was introduced by a blessing of light ("lucernarium") and included psalmody and prayers. (134)

One of the oldest hymns of Christendom, the *Phos Hilaron* or "O Gracious Light," comes from this evening service. The *Phos Hilaron* was sung when candles were lighted for evening prayer, and Basil the Great (379 CE) spoke of singing this ancient hymn as "one of the cherished traditions of the church" (138). For Anglicans, the hymn appears in the evening service:

O gracious Light,
pure brightness of the everliving Father in heaven,
O Jesus Christ, holy and blessed!

Now as we come to the setting of the sun,
and our eyes behold the vesper light,
we sing your praises, O God: Father, Son, and Holy Spirit.

You are worthy at all times to be praised by happy voices,
O Son of God, O Giver of life,
and to be glorified through all the worlds.

This is our oldest, most beautiful hymn, reflecting the light of God. Christians have other references to light in biblical passages and prayers that have been known for centuries. Let's look at some of these, and at three light meditations: candlelight, ball of fire, and chandelier.

Light passages and prayers. Light passages appear in the gospels of the New Testament, and also in Old Testament psalms. Some of these are used in the Anglican prayer book, for services of evening prayer:

Jesus said: You are the light of the world. A city built on a hillside cannot be hid. (Mt 5:14)

Jesus said, I am the light of the world; whoever follows me will not walk in darkness, but will have the light of life. (Jn 8:12)

If I say, 'Surely the darkness will cover me, and the light around me turn to night,' even the darkness is not dark to you; the night is as bright as the day; for darkness is as light to you. (Ps 139:11, 12)

A number of Anglican prayer book prayers are also filled with light:

Lighten our darkness, we beseech thee, O Lord; and by thy great mercy defend us from all perils and dangers of this night; for the love of thy only Son, our Savior, Jesus Christ. Amen.

Almighty God, we give you thanks for surrounding us, as daylight fades, with the brightness of the vesper light; and we implore you of your great mercy that, as you enfold us with the radiance of this light, so you would shine into our hearts the brightness of your Holy Spirit; through Jesus Christ our Lord. Amen.

These are beautiful prayers and passages, reminding us of what Jesus told the early believers so long ago: "God is light, and in him is no darkness at all." Light is part of our Christian heritage, living through Jesus and into the centuries. John tells us: "What has come into being in him was life, and the life was the light of all people. The light shines in the darkness, and the darkness did not overcome it" (1:3–5).

Candlelight. Meditation on a candle flame is an open kind of prayer. I meditate sitting on my pillows, with a lighted candle in front of me. Sometimes my animals like to gather around and be near the light. It's good to use a white candle, as other colors can be heavy or distracting. An unscented candle is better than scented for the same reasons. You may wish to place a few flowers, incense, or a seashell next to your candle.

As the candle burns, simply transfer its light inside you—moving the flame from the floor to the innermost part of your heart as you visualize it. Let it sit in your heart: close your eyes, or close them halfway, and experience the quiet flame burning in your heart. Many of us light candles for people in need or for those who die, but this candle is just for you—part of your present time. When you feel yourself distracted by thoughts, move your attention gently back to the flame. No words are necessary; just let the light shine. The flame may come and go, or leave a feeling of warmth in your heart and body. This is the light of God, shining in and for you.

Ball of fire. The "ball of fire" is another way of looking at light, this time in connection with places in your body needing to be healed. Imagine a small, warm, bright ball of fire in the area of your forehead. Let this ball of light and warmth settle within you. When you're ready, allow the ball of fire to move to parts of your body that are worn, tired, aching, in need of healing. Let it move throughout you, to one part after another: eyes, mouth, ears, top of the head; throat, neck, chest, lungs, heart; arms and hands; stomach, intestines, liver, appendix, genitals; upper legs, knees, ankles, feet, toes.

Let the ball of warmth gently massage and heal as it travels through your body: you may wish to call this the light of Christ, or the light of God, but there's no need to give it a name at all. It can just be a quiet companion, pulsing along with your breathing, allowing you space and time to slow down your thoughts and focus on the light inside. After a while it may even disappear, leaving you feeling calm and refreshed. You can visualize your body in this way at any time, even before you sleep.

Chandelier. This light meditation comes from an experience I had one summer in Berkeley, California. I sat with some Tibetan Buddhists for a week, according to their tradition. We were up every morning at 6:00 to the sound of a gong, and meditation went on until 10:00 every evening. We chanted, did slow meditation exercises, and sat together in silence. During one of the morning exercises before breakfast, I became aware of a multi-tiered glass chandelier, spinning in a central part of my body. I could hear it, like tiny bells, and see it—turning slowly, like the giant prayer wheels the Tibetans use to house their prayers.

This is a good meditation—listening to the chandelier and watching it slowly spin—to remind ourselves that we are filled with light, the clear light of God, at some deep, innermost place. But we will need a good deal of silence to come to this open space. Very slow exercise, for extended periods of time, can help bring us such quiet. Within our inner open space the chandelier never stops; it keeps turning, sending out its light and sound to those ready to see and hear.

These meditations—*breathing, centering prayer, walking, chanting, light*—are contemplative meditations of an open kind. Their openness allows for a good deal of space and silence, taking us to a deeper peace. Some of them will take time to get used to. But as with disciplined practice, first they'll become easier, then second nature. Keep in mind that nothing good happens fast, and *let time take time*. After about a year of regular practice, or even of practicing once or twice a week, you'll find your life slowly changing—less noise, less speed, less distraction, less need to get there and get it done. As Thich Nhat Hanh says: "Peace is every step. We have already arrived" (45).

✒ 3 ✑

Word Prayer

Thousands of words go through our minds every day. They spin and turn like windmills, crowding out the peace and calm living in the silence behind them. We *worry* about the past and *plan* for the future. There seems to be no middle ground, no present moment. Our minds are filled with past longings and future happenings. The French priest François Fénelon, writing in exile around the year 1700, gives us words to remember:

> Try to come before God both in the morning and the evening. Pray during and between all your other jobs as much as you can. You cannot retire too much from the mindless chatter of the world. Learn to steal this time in little snatches, and you will find these moments the most precious part of your day. (75)

Fénelon himself was influenced by Madame Jeanne Bouvier Guyon, imprisoned in the Bastille from 1698 to 1702; her book *Short and Easy Method of Prayer* popularized spiritual disciplines among the laity and was subsequently banned by Rome in 1699. Her ideas were simple and easy to follow; they emphasized living in present time. She called this "beholding the Lord" or "waiting on the Lord":

> Perhaps at this point I need to share with you the greatest
> difficulty you will have in waiting upon the Lord. It has to
> do with your mind. The mind has a very strong tendency
> to stray away from the Lord. (309)

For some of you, the open prayer methods will allow too much
space, and you'll need words to hold onto until you can develop a
greater opening for silence. In the smorgasbord of this section, then,
we'll take a look at three kinds of "word prayers" that have been
with us for a long time: the *Jesus Prayer, Sacred Heart Prayer,* and *Mary
Prayer.* But before we begin, let me tell you a story about a friend
who learned to "label her thoughts," bundling them into groups so
she could begin to remove some of the chatter in her mind.

Watching Thoughts

Joanna Macy—now a well-known author and person of peace—
once told me a story of her trip to Nepal. She climbed high into
the mountains to meet with monks, who were to instruct her in
meditation. They told her to sit alone in a tent and watch her
thoughts. She was to label them accordingly: if she had thoughts of
home, she was to say *home, home, home* in her mind. If she thought
of teaching, she was to say *teaching, teaching* to herself. In this way
she could label her thoughts, summarize them, and let them disappear. Joanna did this for eight hours, in her tent, on her first day in
the mountains.

You may wish to try this meditation yourself. As you watch
your thoughts, you'll see them living in the past and the future. You
can then label them, slow them down, and let them go. They'll
begin to slow like the boats on the river. Or you can substitute the
thoughts for a memorized prayer. Here's a prayer I've used for many
years, from the *Book of Common Prayer:*

> Direct us, O Lord, in all our doings with your most gra-
> cious favor, and further us with your continual help; that
> in all our works begun, continued, and ended in you, we
> may glorify your holy Name, and finally, by your mercy,

obtain everlasting life; through Jesus Christ our Lord. Amen. (BCP 832)

Or this prayer:

O God of peace, who has taught us that in returning and rest we shall be saved, in quietness and in confidence shall be our strength: by the might [mercy] of your Spirit lift us, we pray, to your presence, where we may be still and know that you are God; through Jesus Christ our Lord. Amen. (BCP 832)

My mother and I say this prayer on the phone each evening, before we say goodnight:

O Lord, support us all the day long, until the shadows lengthen, and the evening comes, and the busy world is hushed, and the fever of life is over, and our work is done. Then in your mercy, grant us a safe lodging, and a holy rest, and peace at the last. Amen. (BCP 833)

Throughout the centuries, other chains of prayers have been used to focus the mind on the "inner state of grace," the peace and calm that comes from union with the Holy.

Let's look now at some of these prayers.

Jesus Prayer

The Jesus Prayer belongs to all Christians, but especially to the Orthodox. Near me in the hills of Ohio is a Greek Orthodox monastery. The grounds hold an old white farmhouse, several acres of land, plus a small, round chapel built by the monks. The monks offer spiritual guidance and prayer to those who visit. Michael wears a small wrist cord, a *komvoschinion*, tied with several knots; each knot represents a Jesus Prayer. The words of the prayer are: "Lord Jesus Christ, Son of God, have mercy on me." There are other variations, including "Lord Jesus Christ, have mercy on us" and "Lord Jesus Christ, Son of God, have mercy on me, a sinner."

This prayer is very old; the text of it first appeared in a work of the sixth or seventh century, the life of Abba Philemon. Fifth-century Greek writers such as Diadochus of Photice and Nilus the Ascetic speak of the "remembrance" of the name of Jesus. The Jesus Prayer became deeply influential in the Christian East and was to be prayed constantly, in rhythm with breathing or heartbeat. In later times, and in a text attributed to Simeon the New Theologian (949–1022), a certain physical method was used: head bowed, eyes fixed on the heart, breathing carefully controlled. This practice is now rarely used, but simple breathing is still practiced:

> Lord Jesus Christ (long breath in) have mercy on me (long breath out).

The Jesus Prayer goes back even further, to the biblical stories themselves. In Luke 18:9–14, Jesus tells the parable of the Pharisee and the tax collector. These two men go to the temple to pray. The Pharisee says, "I fast twice a week; I give a tenth of all my income," while the tax collector stands far off, beats his breast and says "God, be merciful to me, a sinner!" We're reminded also of the stories of the blind men and their shout: "Have mercy on us!"

Kallistos Ware, scholar and bishop of the Orthodox Church, says that four main elements can be distinguished in the Jesus Prayer: (1) devotion to the *name of Jesus*, as a source of power and grace; (2) an appeal for *divine mercy*, accompanied by a sense of compunction or grief; (3) the discipline of *frequent repetition*; and (4) the quest for *inner silence* or stillness—*hesuchia*—for imageless prayer (*Study* 176).

This prayer was said throughout the centuries by Orthodox monks, and was often cited thousands of times daily by one person alone. The prayer sometimes distilled down to the recitation of *"Lord Jesus"* or *"Lord, have mercy,"* as in the *kyrie eleison* of our liturgy. Ware mentions the popularity of the Jesus Prayer today among religious and lay persons alike, but cautions that it is not to be thought of as a "Christian mantra":

> The Jesus Prayer is not simply a rhythmic incantation, but an invocation addressed directly to the person of Jesus

Christ. . . .It is not, however, a form of discursive meditation upon particular incidents in Christ's life, but has as
its aim to bring us to the level of *hesuchia* or stillness—to
a state of intuitive, non-discursive awareness in which we
no longer form pictures in our mind's eye or analyse con-
cepts with our reasoning brain, but feel and know the
Lord's immediate presence in a direct personal encounter.
(183–84)

The Jesus Prayer is sometimes also called "the prayer of the
heart" and can be said anytime, anywhere. It not only brings to remembrance our Lord and his mercy, but also helps us align ourselves with centuries of Christian people who have used this simple
prayer to take them to a deeper silence; a deeper peace. This prayer,
in practice, makes us one with a communion of believers stretching
back hundreds of years. Its special joy, according to St. Hesychius
(eighth to ninth centuries), is the sense of sweetness and light it
brings to the heart:

> The more the rain falls on the earth, the softer it makes it;
> similarly, the more we call upon Christ's Holy Name, the
> greater the rejoicing and exultation that it brings to the
> earth of our heart. (*Study* 183)

Sacred Heart Prayer

I first learned of devotions to the Sacred Heart from my spiritual
director and good friend, Rhoda Nary. Rhoda was a devout
Roman Catholic and taught me the prayer she had known from
childhood: "*O Sacred Heart of Jesus, I put my trust in you.*" Or: "*O
Sacred Heart of Mary, I put my trust in you.*" The prayer can be used
with breathing:

> O Sacred Heart of Jesus (long breath in) I put my trust in you
> (long breath out).

This simple prayer is unfortunately associated with the bleeding
hearts of Jesus and Mary: with pictures of the heart surrounded by

thorns and pierced by a sword or spear—the lance of the crucifixion. But bleeding hearts and bad art aside, this is a most helpful prayer. You can meditate on the sorrow of Jesus' or Mary's heart and think of your own sorrow. You can also meditate on *mercy*: the great mercy that Jesus' heart held for others, throughout his own pain, and the sorrow and mercy of Mary, standing at the foot of the cross.

The prayer holds more than sorrow and mercy, though: it's a prayer of *trust*, a call for all of us knowing sorrow and needing help to put our trust in Jesus. For he bore the unbearable—as did his mother, in her sorrow—and yet both knew joy again. The Acts of the Apostles tells us that after Jesus' death, Mary devoted herself to prayer in an upstairs room in Jerusalem, along with the remaining disciples, including women followers and Jesus' brothers (1:12–14).

The Sacred Heart Prayer has its roots in French Catholic spirituality of the seventeenth century, with John Eudes and Margaret Mary Alacoque. But its roots go back even further, to Francis de Sales (b. 1567) and Cardinal Pierre de Berulle (b. 1575), also of the French school. De Berulle, spiritual father for John Eudes, says:

> Let us note that the living heart of Jesus is deeply enough wounded by love. . . . His heart is eternally open, eternally wounded; his glory does not take this wound away, for it is a wound of love; the wound of the lance is only the outward sign of the true and interior wound of his heart. (*Study,* 393)

The first person actually to be associated with both the devotion and its feast day was John Eudes (1601–1680). Eudes was educated by Jesuits, was ordained a priest, and gave noble service during plague years in France; then he spent another ten years conducting missions. He founded the Order of Our Lady of Charity, dedicated to the heart of Mary, to care for "fallen women." He then founded the Congregation of Jesus and Mary, dedicated to the hearts of Mary and Jesus, for priests who taught seminary. But his devotion to the Sacred Heart remained without much response until the visions of Margaret Mary Alacoque (1647–1690).

Margaret Mary (Marguerite Maria) suffered an unhappy childhood; for years she was unable to leave her bed, and she also suffered from an unsympathetic family. But at age 14, having been cured of her illness, she decided to become a nun. At Visitation Convent in Paray-le-Monial she became not just a nun, but later Novice Mistress and Assistant Superior. During this time, 1673–1676, she received several revelations of the Sacred Heart of Jesus.

As has happened to others who became saints, her visions were treated with contempt by her superiors; they thought them simply delusions. But her Jesuit confessor, Claude de la Colombière, told her to record her visions. Her revelations continued to inspire resistance and disbelief within her community, but her confessor supported her until his death in 1682. It is interesting that devotion to the Sacred Heart was not recognized until seventy-five years after Margaret Mary's death. The Jesuits in France became its most ardent supporters.

This devotion, according to some, is traced back to the cult of the Wound in the Side, which now seems to be lost in history. But the Sacred Heart has remained as one of the most popular Roman Catholic devotions, despite the artwork that grew up around it. There is something deeply satisfying about praying to the heart of Jesus, that it may become our own heart, and that we may understand both his sorrow and his mercy. St. Augustine speaks of the Sacred Heart as a "life-giving fountain:"

> O sacred Heart of Jesus! Living and life-giving fountain of eternal life, infinite treasure of the Divinity, glowing furnace of love! You are my refuge and my sanctuary. O my adorable and loving Saviour! Consume my heart with that fire where yours is ever inflamed; pour down on my soul those graces which flow from your love, and let my heart be so united with yours that my will may be conformed to yours in all things. Amen. (*St. Augustine*, 242)

John Eudes and Margaret Mary Alacoque both knew sorrow— he in his mission work among diseased and prostituted women, she with her own ill health and constant rejection. Their prayer is one for times of trial, and also for times of calm and joy; it creates a balance between the suffering and the joy of living. Whether you choose the word "Jesus" or "Mary" in the prayer, the Sacred Heart may also be your own. The Heart holds love, sorrow, joy, and peace.

Mary Prayer

I've had a number of encounters with Our Lady and call her very dear, although I was not raised in a tradition using Mary's devotions. I knew nothing of the *Hail Mary, Salve Regina, Angelus,* or *Memorare,* all ancient prayers revering the mother of our Lord. But Mary has found her way to me any number of times—both in happiness and in sorrow—and I have come to think of her as a companion, as one who protects and watches out for her children here on earth.

Hail Mary. My first encounter with Mary was some twenty years ago, when a close friend died. Emil called one night to say he was having a heart attack, and my husband and I rushed to a hospital to see him. We waited a long time, only to be told he had "arrested" in the ambulance and was rerouted to another hospital. During all this time of rushing, wondering, and waiting, I began to say the *Hail Mary.* I didn't know the prayer, hadn't read it or said it, and there it was:

> Hail, Mary, full of grace; the Lord is with you.
>
> Blessed are you among women, and blessed is the fruit
> of your womb, Jesus.
>
> Holy Mary, Mother of God, pray for us sinners, now
> and at the hour of our death. Amen.

The prayer rolled out of me as if I'd known it all my life. At the hospital, Emil came back briefly to the world, but he later died in the early morning hours. I was not able to see him again, but the Mary Prayer stayed with him through the long night.

I also discovered an old sterling silver rosary one day, at a fleamarket in the Georgetown area of Washington, D.C. The dealer said he "couldn't get rid of the thing" and sold me the beautiful rosary for ten dollars. After that, I came upon an old statue of Mary, hidden away on the grounds of a large statuary dealer. She was cracked, covered with moss and dirt, but her face held a sublime look of peace. I carried her home, and she's been in my gardens ever since, with candles at her feet.

Salve Regina. Soon after the *Hail Mary*, the silver rosary, and the grey-moss statue, I heard the *Salve Regina* for the first time. I sometimes went on retreat to Holy Cross Abbey, a Trappist monastery in Berryville, Virginia. Retreatants were allowed to attend Offices—times of prayer—in the chapel, where the monks would sing and pray. The first evening that I went, at dusk, the monks sang a haunting plainsong: I had never heard anything like it. I later found it was the *Salve Regina*, or the "Hail, holy queen":

> Hail, holy queen, Mother of Mercy; hail, our life, our sweetness, and our hope! To thee do we cry, poor, banished children of Eve; to thee do we send up our sighs, mourning and weeping in this vale of tears. Turn then, most gracious advocate, thine eyes of mercy toward us; and after this, our exile, show unto us the fruit of thy womb, Jesus! O clement! O loving! O sweet Virgin Mary!

I felt I'd been listening to this hymn of praise my entire life. Evening after evening, I went back to hear the monks end services with this beautiful song.

The *Salve Regina* has an interesting story. According to Kevin Orlin Johnson's *Rosary: Mysteries, Meditations, and the Telling of the Beads*, the hymn "seems to have been written by at least two people almost at once" (176). It's attributed to an eleventh-century Benedictine monk, Herman the Cripple, and also to Peter of Monsoro, Bishop of Compostela in Spain (d. 1003). Yet other possible authors are Adhemar, Bishop of Le Puy, who wrote the hymn as a "warsong" of the First Crusade, and Bernard of Clairvaux (1090–1153), the great Cistercian abbot (*Rosary* 176–177). Regardless of its true author, the *Salve Regina* remains a much-loved, ancient hymn of Mary.

Angelus and Memorare. Besides the *Hail Mary* and the *Salve Regina*, I also learned the *Angelus* and the *Memorare*. I knew from *The Angelus*, a painting of peasants stopping in a field to pray, that bells had rung at noon during the Middle Ages. But what was the *Angelus*? Was it the same as the *Hail Mary*? Actually, it was both earlier and longer. The *Angelus* took a long time to develop and was a series of versicles and responses, with a repetitive line: *"Hail, Mary, full of grace; the Lord is with thee."* Peasants recited this prayer at dawn, noon, and dusk all across Europe. Kevin Johnson tells us:

> People who couldn't recite the whole *Angelus*—little children, for instance, or invalids, or people in remote areas who couldn't read it and hadn't been taught it—would simply pause and repeat that Bible verse three times, raising their minds and hearts to God in meditation on the Incarnation as they did. (*Rosary* 31)

As centuries passed other verses were added, including Elizabeth's greeting at the Visitation of Mary: "blessed are you among women, and blessed is the fruit of your womb" (cf. Lk 1:28, 42). By the eleventh and twelfth centuries, these verses were commonly known. The *Angelus* was a devotional prayer, used by simple people throughout their working day. They said prayers according to monastery bells, ringing out at first light, at high noon, and at sunset, as well as at two other times between. In fact, the *Angelus* was so basic to medieval life that it was the main reason parish churches came to be built with bell towers (*Rosary,* 32).

The *Memorare* I learned through my friend Karin, an Anglican. Karin had formerly been Roman Catholic, and she had not forgotten this prayer she learned as a child:

> Remember, O most gracious Virgin Mary, that never was it known that anyone who fled to your protection, implored your help, or sought your intercession was left unaided. Inspired by this confidence, we fly unto you, O Virgin of virgins, our Mother! To you we come, before you we stand, sinful and sorrowful. O Mother of the Word

incarnate, despise not our petitions, but in your mercy hear and answer us. Amen.

Karin wrote down this prayer from memory one day when we were at church. She told me she said the prayer whenever she was worried, anxious, or needed help. Mary, she felt, was someone to count on. Indeed, the prayer has been a widely used intercession, going back centuries, although the *Memorare* wasn't actually in writing until the late fifteenth century—and then as part of a much longer prayer to the Blessed Virgin Mary.

That these ancient prayers of Mary—the *Hail Mary*, the *Salve Regina*, the *Angelus*, the *Memorare*, and others—would survive for hundreds of years, is a testament to their simplicity and beauty, and to the devotion of the people to Mary. Our Lady has long been known as one who protects and intercedes for our suffering. Lawrence S. Cunningham speaks of Mary's power:

> While official Catholic theology has always made a sharp distinction between the *adoration* of God and the *veneration* of the Virgin, the popular piety of the various ages perceived Mary as an all-powerful woman who could demand, as she did in the twelfth century, sanctuaries like the great Gothic cathedrals of Chartres, Paris, and Amiens to honor her. (*Catholic Faith* 136)

Mary's popularity is unparalled in Christian history, and even in a new millennium we still sing her ancient songs.

Rosary. The Rosary has been prayed for a long time, in various forms, by the devout and the poor of the church. Different patterns of this prayer has come together by the end of the fifteenth century and were defined into the rosary by Dominican monk Alan de Rupe (aka Alan de la Roche), born in Brittany. Two hundred years passed before anybody knew what de Rupe had done for the rosary:

> As his fellow Dominicans had done so often in the past, Alan de Rupe had carefully studied all of the various bead-

counted Rosaries that had been prayed for so long all over Europe, but unlike his predecessors he hadn't just condensed these devotions: he had crystallized them. He had reduced the devotion to those common elements that were common to them all. . . (*Rosary,* 49)

De Rupe's rosary is a series of fifteen decades of beads, and the word *bead* itself actually means prayer—coming from the Old English word *biddan.* Saying the Rosary, or "telling the beads," was done for centuries by the faithful of the church:

The Angles, the Saxons, and their joint progeny were particularly fond of bead-counted devotions, but all through Christendom this practice stood as the basis of prayer-lives of the poor. It was particularly dear to the hearts of the country folk who lived in the lands around monasteries. (*Rosary,* 18)

Rosary prayer begins with the *Apostle's Creed,* followed by the *Our Father* and three *Hail Mary*s; concluding with a final *Our Father.* Then one proceeds to pray around the rosary, three times around the five decades of beads. One *Hail Mary* for each of the small beads of the decade, and one *Our Father* between each decade. Each series of five decades is a Mystery: the *Joyful, Sorrowful,* and *Glorious Mysteries.* Each Mystery is then broken down into five meditations, using a variety of scenes from scripture. Traditionally, the *Joyful Mysteries* are said on Mondays and Thursdays; the *Sorrowful Mysteries* on Tuesdays and Fridays, and the *Glorious Mysteries* on Wednesdays and Saturdays. On Sundays, all the Mysteries can be said.

For beginners, the thought of saying an entire rosary can be overwhelming. But its intent is not to be complicated, and learning the rosary just takes practice. The trick of the beads is praying on two different levels: one, saying the *Hail Mary*s themselves, and two, meditating on each Mystery as the decades unfold. I now own two rosaries, one with silver beads and and another crystal beads, but the kind of rosary you have really doesn't matter. Any rosary will work, according to Johnson:

Rosary beads don't have to be made of jewels like the beads
of Lady Godiva, and they don't have to be made of crystal
or precious metal. A rosary can be made of the simplest materials—wood, clay, glass, anything durable enough to stand
up to years of daily wear. It's suitable to have a rosary as
beautifully worked as you can manage, because that's appro-
priate to something made for God's service. . . (*Rosary,* 125)

All the prayers of Mary are "made for God's service," and for
centuries these have deeply touched the hearts of common folk.
Perhaps every time we hear a ringing bell, we can remember the
incarnation in our hearts, as did the faithful in fields near monasteries, generations long ago.

The prayers we have just considered—those to *Jesus,* the *Sacred
Heart,* and *Mary*—have been passed to us through the ages. Behind
each one is a rich history, now mostly forgotten. But how can we
forget this, our heritage? How can we forget the generations
bowing before us, reciting the prayers, asking for God's mercy and
love? These prayers are like the keel of a ship: they hold us in the
water, balance us, and head us in the right direction. They point
the way to the holy.

৵ 4 ৶

Visual Prayer

Lastly we come to visual meditation, prayer using images rather
than words. We have now taken a look at: Jesus' prayer, open prayer,
and word prayer. But visual prayer is something else. I'm always in-
trigued, when teaching centering prayer, by some participants who
resist the idea of a "sacred word." They don't want words. They
want pictures, or images. This is how their minds work, sending
messages and images on the film screens in their heads.

Some people pray better with pictures than words; then they don't have to think about the meaning of words. In my own experience, if a friend is ill, I tend not to say word prayers. Instead, I visualize that part of the friend's body needing healing: the head, lungs, chest, heart, legs, or arms. I send healing light into the body, and that becomes my prayer. One friend of mine calls this prayer a "shield of light," something we can do for one another.

But what can we do for ourselves? What kinds of visual prayer can we try, using images rather than thoughts or words? A number of options are available to us, including: *biblical meditation, icon* and *sacred symbol meditation*, and visualization of *safe places*. Some of these are tried and true meditations, and a few are my own. Visual prayer, as with the other kinds of prayer, is a smorgasbord to choose from: take what you like, or try something new!

Biblical Meditation

In section I we looked at a number of healing stories, but there are other New Testament stories available to us—the parables and miracles, for instance. The *parables* were small stories that Jesus told to his listeners to emphasize a central point: *be ready*, for the kingdom is coming. At heart, the original parables told by Jesus were very simple stories. Some of the most beloved use ordinary, familiar images: *lost sheep* or *coins* (Mt 18:12–14; Lk. 15:1–10), a *seed*, a *growing tree*, and *expanding yeast* (Mt 13:31–33; Mk 4:30–32; Lk 13:18–21).

We also have *miracle stories* to use in our visual meditation. Besides stories of Lazarus, the widow's son at Nain, and Talitha, daughter of Jairus, the gospels give us the *stilling of the storm* (Mt 8:23–27; Mk 4:35–41; Lk 8:22–25); the *walking on water* (Mt 14:22–33; Mk 6:45–52); the *feeding of 5,000* (Mt. 14:13–21; Mk 6:30–44; Lk 9:10–17) and the *feeding of 4,000* (Mt 15:32–39; Mk 8:1–9). Any of these stories can be used for quiet meditation.

A simple process to use with parables or miracles, is this: (1) *listening* to the story—hear it read; (2) *visualizing* the story—let pictures pass through your mind; (3) *meditating* on the sights and sounds of the story; (4) *going deep* with the story. Your image may change into emotion or feeling, or take you to another place. Don't worry if things change; just let the shifting images settle and take you to a place of quiet. Stay in that quiet place until you're ready to return. The image will be your support line, as you descend into a deeper well.

Stilling of the storm. Let's take a look at stories for possible use. The *stilling of the storm* (Mk 4:35–41) is a good one, speaking of something we all can understand: *fear.* In this story, Jesus and the disciples leave a large crowd behind, get into a boat, and begin to cross the water. A great windstorm rises, and waves "beat into the boat," swamping it. Jesus is so exhausted from the day that he's sleeping on a cushion in the stern. The disciples wake him to demand: "Teacher, do you not care that we are perishing?" Jesus then "rebukes" the wind and says to the sea: "Peace! Be still!"

This is a wonderful story for meditation, as there are so many details and so much emotion. I recently used this in a group meditation, and afterward one woman said she stayed with the story for a while, then was carried off to a small garden bench where she used to sit as a child. She sat on her bench, where she felt deep calm and peace. This is very interesting, as Mark 4:39 says: "Then the wind ceased, and there was a dead calm."

The lost coin. This little parable in Luke 15:8–10 is sometimes overlooked, as it comes between two longer stories, of the *lost sheep* and the *lost son.* We have in this story ten silver coins, and one of them has been lost. The woman who has lost the coin lights a lamp and sweeps her house, searching for the coin. She then finds it, calling her neighbors to "rejoice" with her. The small story ends with: "Just so, I tell you, there is joy in the presence of the angels of God over one sinner who repents."

This is a truly wonderful story for meditation: we have a shining lamp, a sorrowful woman, a sweeping broom, and silver coins. We also have joy. If the *stilling of the storm* centers on fear and peace, this story centers on finding and being found. Perhaps it's the light, or the shine of the coins in this story that makes it so attractive, or perhaps it's that all of us know what it feels like to be found. *Joy* is the great emotion in this small story.

The ten bridesmaids. We have another intriguing story, in Matthew 25:1–13, with more lighted lamps and wonderful pictures: ten young women in their beautiful wedding dresses, going out at night with their shining lamps to meet the groom. Five of these women are wise, five are foolish; they all fall asleep, and their oil runs out. The wise maidens have flasks of extra oil, and are prepared to go to the wedding banquet when the bridegroom finally comes. The point, as Luke summarizes it in 12:35–36, is: "Be dressed for action and have your lamps lit. . ."

Although this story is a fierce warning about God's kingdom coming, many images are still available to us for a visual meditation. And there are particulars that we all can understand and have experienced: being foolish and being wise, and watching for the Lord in our lives. The story tells us to "keep awake. . .for you know neither the day nor the hour." The bridesmaids asleep on the dark roadside, with their burning lamps, can also take us to a deeper place.

The mustard seed, a tree, and yeast. We have a couple of tiny stories in Luke 13:18–21, all having to do with the coming kingdom of God. A mustard seed grows in a garden (a "field," in St. Matthew), and becomes a tree ("the greatest of all shrubs" in St. Mark). This tree puts forth large branches, so that the "birds of the air" make nests in them. Following this, a woman takes yeast and mixes it in with "three measures of flour," until all the flour is leavened, and thus grows larger.

The kingdom of heaven is growing, these parables say, right in your midst: seed to tree, with room for birds; and yeast to flour to a round loaf of bread. It's taking place *now*, the story says. We have many visual images here to use in meditation, especially the birds and their nests. The tree "puts forth large branches so that the birds of the air can make nests in its shade" (Mk 4:32). This story gives a feeling of safety and protection, and a feeling of growth; the round bread also speaks of God's kingdom growing, becoming larger. All of the stories speak of God's kingdom being with us in present time.

Any of these parables and miracles is good for visual meditation—they are wonderful stories, filled with pictures and emotions we can understand. Or you could choose other stories, equally compelling, such as the *treasure in a field* and the *pearl of great price* (Mt. 13:44–46). Watch these stories in your mind, as if you're seeing them filmed, and let them take you down to a quiet place. They are all treasures and pearls, shining lamps and coins, leading us to the kingdom of God surrounding us right now. As Luke 17:21 says: "The kingdom of God is among you."

Icons

Icons are another visual way to take us down into deep quiet; they have been called "windows to heaven." They're especially revered in Orthodox Christianity. *Icon* (Latin) or *eikon* (Greek) simply means "likeness" or "image," and icons are pictures of Mary, Jesus, saints, and angels. The pictures are flat, usually painted in egg tempera on wood or wood panels, but they're also made of ivory or precious materials. They may also be mosaic or fresco on walls (*Study,* 197).

Icons have recently come back into popularity among Christians, but they've had a long and complicated history in the church. The pictures have been numerous in the East since the fifth century, and the Orthodox claim they were used from the time of the early disciples. Icons were used devotionally, as prayers themselves, and some became famous for miracles:

> As it is believed that through them the saints exercise their beneficent powers, they preside at all important events of human life and are held to be effective remedies against illness, to drive away devils, to procure both spiritual and temporal blessings, and generally to be powerful channels of Divine grace. (*Oxford,* 815)

Then came the great "Iconoclastic Controversy" on the veneration of icons, which continued in the Greek Church from 725 to 842. Some of the emperors in Constantinople began to destroy revered icons: Emperor Leo III (717–741) thought that the excessive use of icons was a main obstacle for the conversion of both Jews and Muslims. In 726 he published an edict "declaring all images idols and ordering their destruction" (*Oxford,* 815). Persecutions and hostilities followed, especially against monks who defended devotion to icons.

The controversy involved theological and political disputes between East and West, and among Christians, Muslims, and Jews. *Iconoclasts* wanted the paintings removed from churches, while *iconodules* argued that icons of Christ made the incarnation legitimate. In 787 the Seventh General Council, meeting at Nicea, said icons were "a guarantee that the incarnation of God the Word is true and not "illusory'" (*Study,* 196). This Council overturned previous councils, redefined veneration to icons, and restored their place in Christianity.

For the Orthodox, icons are a liturgical art—not just pieces of devotional decoration, but actual parts of the liturgy. In this sense they fulfill a sacramental function, as channels of divine grace. They bring us to the presence of God, and to the saints:

> By virtue of the icon the worshipper enters the dimensions
> of sacred time and space, and so is brought into a living, ef-
> fectual contact with the person or mystery depicted. The
> icon serves not as a mere reminder only but as a means of
> communion. Surrounding the congregation on every side,
> the icons ensure that the communion of saints is not simply
> an article of faith, but a fact of immediate experience.
> (*Study,* 197)

Icons can also be used in private devotion. In Orthodox households there is traditionally an icon corner or shelf, where lamps are lighted, incense is offered, and family prayers are said. This is thought to be "heaven on earth" (*Study* 198). If you wish to use an icon for meditation, first find one that you'll be comfortable with. Once I was asked to meditate on an icon of the Trinity: three men with dark beards and flowing robes. I couldn't relate to this at all, but I later found a wonderful Black Madonna from Czechoslovakia, a blue and white St. Clare of Assisi, and a brown St. Francis with golden aura about his head. These were simple, wooden icons; I placed a candle beneath them, and let it burn for special intentions.

Personal meditation with icons is very simple: you can place the icon on the floor, on a wall space, or on a nightstand. You may wish to venerate the icon, burn incense, or light it up with a candle. Then you can meditate on the icon's face, allowing its spirit to come into your heart, and allowing you to "see through" to the mystery beyond. The central focus is the face, not the life of the person. Allow the meditation to become a visual experience: "Through the liturgical art of the icon, God is experienced not only as truth and love but also as *beauty*" (*Study* 198).

One other word: when you meditate on an icon, don't be surprised if the form changes. The face may shift, become lighter or darker; reveal deep sorrow or deep happiness. Rather than analyze or become distracted, just be present with the icon. Keeping eyes half-open may be helpful, or even after a while closing your eyes. Icons are meant to be transcendent, a true "heaven on earth" where we are transported from time and place into a living, visual sphere. Allow them to breathe with you and become alive, as you enter their holy space.

Sacred Symbol Meditation

We've been talking about biblical and icon visual prayer, but there are other visual meditations: some of our own dreaming and drawing. What about pictures of God? I first began drawing "pictures of God" with Shalem groups. On Saturday quiet days we would draw, on large pieces of paper with crayons, our *life lines* (growing up, schooling, marriage, children, jobs), our *spiritual life lines* (callings, changes, whisperings, nudges), and our *pictures of God* (images of the holy as we understood them).

People in one of my first groups made elaborate pictures of God: old men smoking cigars, women in wildly patterned dresses with miles of knotted hair. My first picture was one little stroke in the upper right hand corner—a bird in flight, in a lot of space. Perhaps the space was my picture of God and the bird was me. After all the years of intense seminary training, I needed space and simplicity. God seemed spacious to me.

Over the years I drew many pictures, and they always changed. One time I drew some sheep, white but angular, munching on green grass. I never tried to read into my pictures; I just let them happen. Another time I drew a long green pine in sunlight. If I had to draw a picture of God now, I might draw a lighted candle sitting on a stone, next to a lily pond. "Be here now," Ram Dass said, and that's where "God" is: right here, right now.

This little experiment is not only an exercise in imagination, but also an exercise in your own trust and faith. Maybe God isn't anywhere for you right now. Draw that. Maybe God or the Spirit or your Higher Power is everywhere, so that you can just stand on a bridge and sing. Draw that, standing and singing. Draw on blue paper, white paper, yellow paper, or green paper. Tear it up and move it around. Let your pictures jump out of the box. Hang them on a branch of a tree, on your rear-view mirror, or tape them to your ceiling.

All of these things are symbol. Christianity has a long history of symbol—something that stands for something else. But maybe it's more than that. Maybe, like an icon, a sacred symbol has a life of its own, moves beyond our definitions, takes us to a greater silence and greater peace. In Christianity, we have *crosses* and *crucifixes* for our Lord's sacrifice; *fish* drawn on caves, where early Christians met in secret; *lambs* for the Lamb of God; *three intertwined rings* for the Holy Trinity; *white doves* for the Holy Spirit; *Alpha* and *Omega* for beginning and end.

Besides these, we Christians also have outward *signs* of the sacraments: the *water* of baptism, *bread* and *wine* of the Eucharist (going beyond symbol!), the *oil* of unction for healing, the *sign of the cross* for penance, *exchanged rings* and *tied knots* for marriage, *candles* for confirmation and baptism, and the wearing of priests' and deacons' *stoles* for ordination. We also have *bells* at the consecration during the Eucharist, and *incense* for censing and the rising of our prayers. Or perhaps you have other objects you'd like to use in symbol meditation. I recently attended a class where we brought in symbols: one for what God was doing in the present moment; another for how we were responding to that; and one for "what would we be like, when the work of the Lord was done." I brought in a blue meditation pillow, a pink seashell for listening, and a vial of jasmine oil for being healed and healing. Try this little exercise, without thinking about it: what three symbols would you bring in?

Once you try this and find your symbols, use them visually to inspire you to a deeper peace. Sit with your shell for a while, or walk around with it in your hand. Hang it on your mirror. Let it stay next to you at night, as a comfort and a place of rest. Our symbols are powerful, needing to be experienced. They represent something holy for us, something sacred, and if we let them be, that holiness will come to us in a deep quiet way.

Pictures of God or how we experience God, traditional Christian symbols, or our own sacred symbols: give them all a try. Our task now, living in our radically changed world, is to bring ourselves to a greater peace. Whenever, however, we begin, this process is vital to us all—*finding peace*, then passing it on, from one human being to another. Sacred symbols will stay with us, reminding us of the presence of the holy in our daily lives.

Safe Places

Jesus said: "Come to me, all you that are weary and are carrying heavy burdens, and I will give you rest. . . .For my yoke is easy, and my burden is light" (Mt 11:28, 30). We all need to find this great rest, and sometimes we can find it in our safe places. In meditation groups I have met so many people trying to find *home* again: whether it's strawberry fields on a farm in Virginia, a wooden bench in a secret childhood garden, or my mother's roses next to an old white garage. These are our safe places: those times from childhood when all was right with the world—no bombs, no death threats, no assassinations, no terrorists. Just safe places of the heart.

Now let me take you on a journey, a visual meditation to an old farmhouse belonging to my grandmother. Laila's home was a beautiful 1830s Western Reserve house in Ohio, on old farmland property; it had belonged to her Uncle Theo before it belonged to her. The house sat by the railroad tracks of a middle-sized town, on Portage Trail East, where Native Americans had carried their canoes up and down to the river. Close your eyes for a while; imagine you're there.

Imagine that you're visiting Laila's house—a beautiful old white country house, with black crisscross windows, a blue-grey roof, and a large verandah—on a sunny summer day. You're standing inside the house now, in the large entrance hall with its white brick fireplace. You can see the narrow winding staircase at the end of the hall. You walk slowly through the entrance hall, and look through the archway to the open living room windows: you see the verandah and long, green lawns leading down to ponds. No one else is nearby, and it's a very quiet day. You hear birdsong outside and see sunlight all around.

You move slowly through a side door and out onto the wide verandah. You see plants and ferns, white wood lattices, green and white striped awnings with ropes, and Laila's old porch swing on chains. You sit in the swing, resting, and listen to the chains as they jingle and rattle. You breathe and relax, let go, drift deeper and deeper down. You're aware of birds in trees, wooden benches, and long, lovely gardens rolling down both sides of the yard. You breathe and relax, step out into the yard. You take off your shoes and socks, and walk slowly through the grass.

You're feeling very relaxed now, sinking deeper into inner peace. You wander slowly through the grasses and see ponds—one rectangular pond and two small round ponds—opening up in front of you. You've heard that your grandfather built these ponds from cement, when he moved the house with donkeys up to higher ground. You marvel at the age of the ponds, their shine, how much life they house: green lilies with yellow blooms, strings of sticky frog eggs, water bugs, spiders, black tadpoles, orange fish, green algae, smooth stone. You stop to feel the stone.

You move on, slowly, to the flowers: tall pink gladiolas and yellow daylilies, lavender and yarrow, asters and coneflowers, and black-eyed susans. Rows and rows of colors, smells, blooming flowers. You see, to your left, a large white arbor holding grapevines; the vines tangle and turn on the wood, creating an inner space of calm and quiet. You walk inside the arbor, a dark moist tunnel blocking out the light; you smell the sweetness of grapes even though they haven't yet arrived. You're safe here, with the grapes and vines; the safest you've ever been.

Now you're back outside, in the sunlight again. You can breathe, walk peacefully, enjoy the warmth of the sun. You find yourself standing by a fish pond, looking down. You sit and rest, trailing your hand in the water, pulling green weed along the surface. You find a bright penny, and drop the coin in the water. You see it ripple down, flash slowly through the water. It drifts deeper and deeper, falls into soft mud at the bottom of the pond. You watch the fish—orange and red and gold—the tadpoles, the lilies. You feel the sun. You're at peace, like the penny in the pond, resting on the bottom. You close your eyes. You're safe now, at home. You'll always be at home, in this stillness and peace.

Thank you for traveling with me on a trip to my grandmother's house, gardens, and ponds. You can make this trip any time, or take a trip to your own safe place. Where did you last feel free from all harm? Where did you last know peace? In our hearts, childhood doesn't have to end, and our peaceful places can be many: within our minds, or in our own homes and gardens. We just have to look for them again to reconnect with our safe places of the heart.

We have now journeyed through several types of visual meditation based on *biblical stories, icons, sacred symbols,* and *safe places.* This concludes our survey in Part II of three kinds of contemplative prayer: *open prayer, word prayer,* and *visual prayer.* All of these prayers and meditations lead to that deep well where the mercy and stillness of God abide—that place of rest, our home. Jesus says: "Let anyone who is thirsty come to me. . . .As the scripture has said, 'Out of the believer's heart shall flow rivers of living water'" (Jn 7:37, 38).

*There it was, all round them. . .there is a coherence
in things, a stability; something, she meant, is immune
from change, and shines out (she glanced at the window
with its ripple of reflected lights) in the face of
the flowing, the fleeting, the spectral, like a ruby;
so that again tonight she had the feeling she had
had once today, already, of peace, of rest. Of such
moments, she thought, the thing is made
that remains for ever after.*
—Virginia Woolf, *To the Lighthouse*

III. HEALING PRACTICE

Now we come to the hard part. So far we've taken a look at the healing stories of Jesus, and perhaps you've seen a few you're touched by, identify with, or will remember. We've also viewed a wide variety of contemplative prayer practices, and perhaps in these you've found something appealing; two or three you'd like to try. But the real test of all this is how it relates to our everyday life: how it affects the way we think, feel, and act—if it helps us find peace and healing from one day to the next.

Let me tell you about Paul, a friend and parishioner I met with for spiritual direction. Paul was a businessman: very bright, active in the parish, devoted to his work and family, and very good hearted. But he was having trouble in the workplace. Paul would go to meetings and find himself having two reactions: he would either become angry and blow up at people, or he would acquiesce to everyone and be angry with himself. There seemed to be no middle ground. I asked him if he ever thought of applying the things he heard in church—about peace, love, acceptance—to his situation in the workplace. He said no; it had never occurred to him.

Paul and I talked, then, about taking a moment to *stop*: to stop and breathe, stop and pray, to find a middle way between aggression and caving in. Perhaps there was a way of peace in between the extremes, a way of consensus and understanding—a way of bringing Jesus' light and presence into everyday existence. Paul thought about this and came back a few weeks later to report he had found some middle ground, and now could see more clearly.

Finding this "way in the middle" is not easy. But there are conscious things we can do, choices we can make, to turn our path toward peace. If we can find small points of peace in our lives, these will then spill over—to our work, our families, our friends and neighbors, our world. Watching our responses, practicing our peace and practicing prayer will lead to a different way of living. Dom Thomas Keating says: "The only way to practice this prayer is by its long-range fruits: whether in daily life you enjoy greater peace, humility and charity" (*Open Mind,* 114).

Keating is talking about the "fruits of the Spirit," listed in that much-loved passage from the letter to the Galatians. Before this passage Paul speaks of the *works of the flesh*: "fornication, impurity, licentiousness, idolatry, sorcery, enmities, strife, jealousy, anger, quarrels, dissensions, factions, envy, drunkenness, carousing"— quite a list. Then he gives us the *fruits*:

> By contrast, the fruit of the Spirit is love, joy, peace, patience, kindness, generosity, faithfulness, gentleness, and self-control. There is no law against such things. (Gal 5:22)

Practicing any one of these takes a good deal of time. First, we have to practice our meditation, our contemplation, and if it's deep enough and long enough, the fruits will slowly come.

Let's take a look, then, at putting all this to work. We'll go back through the centuries to see the monastic practice of *rhythm of hours*;

then we'll take a look at St. Benedict's *Rule of Life*. After that we'll look further at *life in the Spirit* on the radical edge, *Sabbath time* in a high-speed world, *reverence for life* and all creation; and *practicing peace* in a world of great unrest. Our world is nothing like it used to be. So we have to look back at our ancestors, to find their wisdom, and look forward, to see what we can see. "For now we see in a mirror, dimly," says Paul, "but then we will see face to face" (1 Cor 13:12).

⚜ 1 ⚜

Rhythm of Hours

When I used to live and work in the Washington, D.C. area, peoples' lives and schedules were jammed: Rush hour lasted from early morning hours to early evening hours. Driving two miles into the city each morning to my job would take one very long hour. The clergy I knew were scheduled several months in advance with special meetings, regular work, and conferences. Some of the nationally known people I worked with at the Shalem Institute scheduled themselves a year in advance. No one seemed to like living this way, but everyone did it. Calendars filled up fast.

We haven't always lived this way, and there was a slower time when bells and sunlight ruled a Christian's life. Let's take a look at some of the practices of those times: how they developed, how they were destroyed, and how they changed to other forms. We'll consider prayers of the hours, the dissolution of monasteries, and the *Book of Common Prayer*.

Prayers of the Hours

If you had lived in a monastery or convent long ago, your day would have revolved around the monastic "offices." *Offices* simply meant "service" or "duty," and within that duty were the "Prayers of the Hours" based on the one hundred fifty psalms. This devotion has its roots in the practice of Jesus' disciples, who gathered to

say prayers at certain times: "They devoted themselves to the apostles' teaching and fellowship, to the breaking of bread and the
prayers" (Acts 2:42; see also 1:14; 3:1; 10:9, 30; and 16:25). These
prayers were a continuation of the Jewish practice, and as they
evolved, they combined the psalms with gospel readings, prophe-
cies, homilies, and penitential chants such as the *kyrie* (*Rosary* 20).

Timekeeping in early Christian and later medieval times followed the ancient Roman practice of dividing daylight, no matter
how long or short, into twelve hours: six hours between dawn and
solar noon, six hours between solar noon and sunset. The
monastery bells rang out at first light, at high noon, at sunset, and
also when the sun was at the halfway mark between dawn and
noon, or between noon and sunset:

> Those five peals marked the major divisions of the twelve
> daylight hours, and five of the canonical hours were set on
> that frame of reference; but there are two canonical hours
> during the night, for a total of seven—'seven times a day I
> praise thee' (Ps 119:164). (*Rosary,* 20)

The Prayers of the Hours came to have certain names: *Lauds* or
Matins at midnight, from "at midnight I rise to praise you" (Ps
119:62). Then followed *Prime* at dawn, *Terce* at the third hour, *Sext*
at solar noon, *None* at the ninth hour, *Vespers* at sunset—for the
name of the evening star—and *Compline* in the evening. Vespers, the
time when candles were lighted and the *Phos Hilaron* said, was also
called *Lucernarium*—lamplighting time (*Rosary,* 21).

All of these hours rotated around light and darkness, sun and
monastery bells, in the time before clocks. People in the fields knew
when to pray, and even the nobility structured their daily schedules
around prayers announced by bells, ringing for the hours. Peoples'
lives were closely connected to the seven monastic hours of the day.

> No two days' hours are exactly alike, and with seven
> canonical hours for each of three hundred and sixty-five
> days, there are more than twenty-five hundred different
> patterns of prayer in the entire devotion. (*Rosary,* 22)

Following the canonical hours came lectionaries, breviaries, and plenaries—lessons to read, instructions on days, and the texts themselves. Thus developed over the years and centuries an exacting system of prayer. This system was more for the "religious"—monks and nuns—than for the laity, who had family duties and ordinary hard labor to attend to. But the laity still observed some of the hours, especially the daylight hours of *Terce, Sext,* and *None,* sometimes called the "Little Hours." These prayers went on—practiced, sung, and said by the faithful—for hundreds of years.

Dissolution of the Monasteries

In the sixteenth century, however, cataclysmic changes came for the church, including destruction of the great monasteries and changes in prayer. The Protestant Reformation began in a whirlwind, with Martin Luther in Germany, Ulrich Zwingli in Switzerland, French reformer John Calvin in Switzerland, and John Knox in Scotland.

In England, also, reform began to take place: Henry VIII broke with Pope Clement VII over annulment of his marriage to Catherine of Aragon, who had not produced a male heir; Henry wanted to marry Anne Boleyn. In 1527 the king began a six-year quest to end the marriage. But Catherine was aunt to Emperor Charles V of the great Spanish Empire; the Pope warned Henry of excommunication if he remarried.

Believing his marriage to Catherine had gone against God's law, Henry joined up with Thomas Cranmer, Archbishop of Canterbury. Anne became pregnant, and in 1533 Henry secretly married her. Cranmer annulled the king's first marriage, and pronounced Anne the valid Queen. Anne gave birth to a daughter, Elizabeth, and the Pope again threatened excommunication unless Henry returned to Catherine.

But Henry pressed on. In 1534 a Succession Act recognized his marriage to Anne, and a Supremacy Act declared Henry "supreme head" of the Church of England. Events followed that changed the English Church to its core: a series of laws severed the bonds between Rome and England, and Henry was excommunicated.

Monks and others denying royal supremacy were executed, and threat of a crusade against England forced the king to find money. The wealth of English monasteries became his focus, and Henry gradually destroyed them. The Suppression of Religious Houses Act was passed in 1536, and the dissolution of monasteries and destruction of shrines began:

> Effected in a brutal and highly unscrupulous manner, the Dissolution of Monasteries met with small resistance. . . . The incidental losses to charity, art, and learning were considerable, many precious manuscripts perishing through destruction and decay. (*Oxford,* 490)

But there was a building resistance to this destruction. In 1536 the Pilgrimage of Grace began in northern counties: a series of risings took place, called by the people "the pilgrimage of grace for the commonwealth." The resistance involved an intense dislike of government dealings in religious matters, plus grievances concerning taxes and landowner's rights. Robert Aske, from an old Yorkshire family, headed a rebellion of 30,000 men.

Henry promised that grievances would be redressed, but by 1537 Aske was seized and made a prisoner in the Tower of London. He was condemned for high treason, and hanged in chains at York. And at Henry's order over two hundred other rebels were also hanged, as a "fearful spectacle" to others (*Oxford,* 1288). The Pilgrimage dissolved, and the spoils of the Dissolution passed from the Crown to Tudor nobility and gentry. England's great monasteries and manuscripts had disappeared, along with generations of faithful prayer.

The Book of Common Prayer

The beginnings of the English Reformation wore on. Under Edward VI—son of Henry and Jane Seymour who came to the throne at age ten—the first (1549) and second (1552) *Books of Common Prayer* were produced by Cranmer. But the Archbishop of Canterbury was himself burned at the stake as a heretic when Mary

Tudor—Catherine's daughter—became Queen after Edward's early death.

Cranmer's prayer books, however, did not disappear, despite Mary's very Roman Catholic reign. Following Mary was Queen Elizabeth I—daughter of Henry and Anne Boleyn—and Protestant sympathies and supporters once again ruled. In 1559 the third *Book of Common Prayer* was fashioned as a compromise for both Catholics and Protestants. Cranmer's Morning and Evening Prayer offices, first penned in 1549, were remnants of the Daily Office of the monks.

To this day the Episcopal Church in the United States retains these Offices in the 1979 *Book of Common Prayer* (BCP). The Daily Office includes: *Daily Morning Prayer, Noonday Prayer, Order of Worship for the Evening* (Vespers), *Daily Evening Prayer,* and *Compline.* The Prayer Book also holds a number of "little offices," or *Daily Devotions for Individuals and Families,* including prayers for morning, noon, early evening, and close of day. These "little offices" are especially good for brief prayer times during the day.

Few people are aware now that the Daily Offices in the Book of Common Prayer are what remain of the seven canonical hours of early and medieval Christianity. Even fewer are aware that Anglicans, Roman Catholics, and Orthodox still have monks and nuns who say the hours daily. People in the church still have access to these beautiful psalms and lessons, whenever we want them. The question for most of us now is: how do we incorporate these prayers into our busy daily lives?

The solution may be as simple as carrying a prayer book throughout the day. We can turn to the little offices and read each service, or just read one prayer. Perhaps on a break from work we can take a moment, and read this morning prayer:

> Lord God, almighty and everlasting Father, you have brought us in safety to this new day: Preserve us with your mighty power, that we may not fall into sin, nor be overcome by adversity; and in all we do, direct us to the fulfilling of your purpose; through Jesus Christ our Lord. Amen. (BCP, 137)

At noon, on a lunch hour or before a short walk, we can read another:

> Lord Jesus Christ, you said to your apostles, 'Peace I give to you; my own peace I leave with you:' Regard not our sins, but the faith of your Church, and give to us the peace and unity of that heavenly City, where with the Father and the Holy Spirit you live and reign, now and for ever. Amen. (BCP, 138)

In the early evening, as the sun is going down, we have this lovely prayer:

> Lord Jesus, stay with us, for evening is at hand and the day is past; be our companion in the way, kindle our hearts, and awaken hope, that we may know you as you are revealed in Scripture and the breaking of bread. Grant this for the sake of your love. Amen. (BCP, 139)

And before we sleep, we can take fifteen minutes to read a prayer, to be in silence with our thanksgiving and prayers of intercession:

> Visit this place, O Lord, and drive far from it all snares of the enemy; let your holy angels dwell with us to preserve us in peace; and let your blessing be upon us always; through Jesus Christ our Lord. Amen. (BCP, 140)

Our hours no longer revolve around sun and bells, or toil in the fields. Prayer has slipped from our lives. We rush to get up, rush to work—leaving spouses, children, parents, animals, plants, and homes behind. We return in the evening, worn from the day, lucky to say a few "God-blesses" as we roll into bed and turn off the light. If we are to pray again, find a rhythm of hours again, perhaps a total realignment of our lives is necessary. Perhaps things we think fundamental will disappear, and other gifts will take their place: silence, serenity, and peace; charity, mercy, and goodwill. But this is a radical notion. We can begin with making a rule of life.

❧ 2 ❧

Rule of Life

During seminary I became an Associate of the Order of Holy Cross (OHC), an Anglican men's religious order in New York. The Order of St. Helena (OSH) was then a women's order affiliated with OHC. St. Helena's became independent in 1975, and I'm now an associate with these wonderful nuns. What does being an associate mean? It means we're asked, as lay or clergy Christians, living in the world, to "undertake a regular commitment to prayer and Christian life." In particular, we're asked to formulate a rule of life.

Rule of St. Benedict

The rule of life in Christianity goes all the way back to Benedict of Nursia (480–550), sometimes called "the father of Western monasticism." But other monastic rules and disciplines preceded Benedict, and he borrowed from them:

> The developments initiated or conveyed by Pachomius, Basil, Jerome, Ambrose, Martin of Tours, the bishops from Lerins, Augustine and above all John Cassian were explicitly or implicitly present in the culture of the numerous monasteries of sixth century Italy and Gaul. (*Study*, 150)

Many believe that the Rule of Benedict was dependent on the somewhat earlier *Anonymous Rule of the Master*, but Benedict's Rule is less than a third of the Master's Rule. Benedict's Rule is some seventy-three chapters.

Little is actually known about Benedict. An account of his life in the second book of *Dialogues* by Gregory the Great is the only reference we have. Benedict was born in Nursia, northeast of Rome, and he died as abbot of Monte Cassino, a monastery midway between Rome and Naples; he is buried there in the grave of his sister,

Scholastica. Apparently he was never ordained, and never had an intention of founding an order.

Benedict was educated in Rome, and in reaction to the moral corruption he found there, he withdrew to live as a hermit in a cave at Subiaco (c. 500), east of Rome. A monastery was nearby, with monks living in community. Benedict lived alone for three years, but followers eventually sought him out. He organized the followers into twelve monasteries, each with twelve monks and an abbot, after Jesus and the disciples.

Benedict directed his monasteries for twenty-five years, until he was driven out by persecution from an "unholy priest" (*Study*, 149). With a small band of loyal monks he moved to Monte Cassino; there he spent seventeen years establishing a monastery, converting "pagans," and writing his Rule. Gregory the Great attributes to Benedict a series of miracles, showing him to be a most holy man of God (*Study*, 150).

Benedict's Rule is addressed to monks living in community, with obedience to an abbot or head monk. The Rule is centered in three great virtues: *obedience, silence*, and *humility*. Vows were not taken by the monks:

> There is no mention of 'vows,' or of the three evangelical counsels, poverty, chastity, or obedience. The practice of taking these vows in religious life was a much later development. (*Study*, 155)

At the heart of the Rule is the Divine Office (*opus dei*), the canonical hours of prayer. Private prayer is hardly mentioned, except for *meditatio* during working hours. The prayer times were interspersed with physical labor (*ora et labora*) for six hours daily and sacred reading (*lectio divina*) for four hours daily. The monks ate and slept in moderation, and Benedict believed they should live by their own labor: the monastery was self-supporting.

Benedict's Rule served for centuries as a measuring rod for monastic communities, and it is still used today. As early as the seventh and eighth centuries, the Rule was widely followed in Gaul, England, and Germany, but Benedictines were not actually known as the Order of St. Benedict (OSB) until other religious orders developed using other names. Throughout the years, laypersons as well as monastics have profited from the Rule:

> . . .there is little or no spirituality in the Rule of Benedict other than monastic spirituality. But because what is there is founded wholly in scripture, it is not surprising that lay folk have profited through the centuries from the spirituality of the Rule and of the life that continues to be lived in monasteries according to the Rule. (*Study,* 156)

Making a Rule of Life

A rule of life is still used in monastic communities today, and the faithful are encouraged to use one in their secular lives as well. The Order of St. Helena, for example, suggests that these traditional categories be used in the formation of a rule: (1) *corporate prayer*, or worship in church; (2) *individual prayer;* (3) *repentance and reconciliation,* using the Sacrament of Reconciliation; (4) *fasting and abstinence,* for instance on Good Friday and Ash Wednesday; (5) *devotional reading of scripture* and *spiritual books*; and (6) *regular giving,* of time, talents, and money, to church and charities.

While this is the structure of a traditional Rule, other rules can be formed. For instance, when I was recently a doctoral student in a local seminary, I was asked in a course to write a ten page paper on my "rule of prayer." At first I couldn't imagine writing a rule of life for ten pages. What would I possibly say? Three or four pages, perhaps, but ten? I thought about all the traditional categories, and how I would begin to expand on them.

But the traditional things didn't really interest me; I knew all my best promises would soon be broken—trying to say offices, attend eucharists, and read books. Instead, I thought large, about areas in my life that have remained constant over the years. I came up with three major areas and wrote about those: (1) *living simply;* (2) *praying;* (3) *caring for creation.* As I wrote about these and came to the end, I suddenly realized I was leaving out a major category in my life: *writing*. So I added a fourth category and continued to write.

Before I began this entire process, I sat down to meditate on an early winter day. After quieting down I started to write:

> *Stillpoint, 4:40 PM, almost twilight.* Breathe in, breathe out. I sit on blue pillows, face open glass doors of my home. Green pines, blue sky, hush of light. Two big dogs fall at my feet and roll in my lap. They want attention. I want silence: peace and quiet, in the middle of stacks of papers, a homily, calls to make, letters to write. I calm down, centering down, thoughts racing: *teaching, teaching, writing, writing, thinking, thinking.* I breathe. I see a waterfall, silver-pure, dropping from a distance. I float, rise, fall with the fall. Where'd this come from? Where's it going? Dogs roll and flop, cats skirmish, the radio's on—low, scratchy music. I get up, yell at cats and dogs, turn off music, sit again. *Breathe in, breathe out.* Quiet now, quiet. Waterfall, fall. Going down, deeper. Quiet. Church bells ringing, 5:00. Time to feed dogs, feed cats. Get mail. Call mother. *I nod to trees, breathe in sky, rise from pillows.*

Following this introduction I wrote through my four areas without stopping. I rolled out twelve pages with ease, and probably could have gone for twelve more. So give this method a try: Think through the areas in your life that are most important, and list them on paper. Then expand on them, adding detail, and begin sketching out your rule of prayer. But whatever you do, don't make your rule so complicated that it's impossible to follow. Keep your expectations low, and stay in reality. What's really possible, and practical, for your daily life?

Perhaps the first thing to consider is how to make your life simpler, so you'll have time for prayer. Think of all the chores you do, all the running around in any given day. Some of these can be consolidated, passed on to others, or assigned a certain day or time. Think of all the time spent watching late-night television, or television during the day. Maybe even larger issues are at hand, like time spent commuting to work. Could the commute become a time for prayer? Or is there another, simpler job, closer by? Living more simply may mean giving up, to find some quiet.

Perhaps you need to consider other things: good health time and physical exercise time. If you begin to open time for prayer in your life, is it also possible to open time for your body, and good health? A daily walk is not only good exercise; it's a wonderful time for prayer. And how about the foods going into your body—lots of animal fat? Junk food? Diet drinks and sugar? Think about the simple foods your body needs.

Our rules don't have to just encompass traditional categories; they can include what we do every day, to lessen our stress and keep ourselves healthy. We can take small steps to change the way we live and find small openings for serenity and prayer. These openings will become larger with time, and our lives will begin to change.

Spiritual Friend

Creating a sensible rule may be hard to do alone. You'll start out with good intent, but after a few weeks or months your interest may wane. That's because you're trying to do it alone, and without a guide to talk with about your experiences. In previous centuries, and especially before the Reformation changed patterns of spirituality, monastics—nuns and monks—had both spiritual directors and confessors. And the laity spoke with their priests, so that everyone who wanted would have a spiritual mentor.

The long practice of spiritual mentoring died out with the Protestant reform, and in the seventeenth century Roman Catholics faced their own controversies. Mystical writings and the mystical tradition were discouraged, no longer taught in seminaries and religious communities (*Open*, 24). But in the last decades of the twentieth century a renewed interest in spirituality began for Anglicans, Romans Catholics, and mainline Protestants. More and more people now—lay and clergy, as well as those outside the church— are looking for a mentor.

I found one or two early spiritual directors through seminary, but I mostly found them through the Shalem Institute. I looked for people older than myself, ahead of me on the spiritual path. My director Rhoda lived in my neighborhood, and we also belonged to a small group that met at her house once weekly. This group of women met for six years, rain or shine, and we saw our lives go through many changes: births, adoptions, deaths, divorce, remarriage, new jobs. We all became fast friends, and prayed our lives together for weeks, months, and years.

I acted as a spiritual director myself, especially for women wanting to be ordained. I didn't seek these people out, but they seemed to find me. I met with them once monthly for an hour at the hospital where I worked. During that time I was also meeting with a beloved priest friend. Darlene and I met monthly for two hours in a small chapel at the Washington National Cathedral and talked about our work, our prayer lives, and our families. The first hour, one of us would talk and the other listen; then we would switch roles. These meetings were a source of great comfort.

But what exactly is spiritual direction, and how do you go about finding someone to meet with? It may be that there is someone in your parish you admire, or a good friend who you share common interests with, or someone you've heard about through others. Ask around and meet with a few people to see who you feel most comfortable with. As the Buddhists say: when you need one, a Teacher will appear. Say a prayer, turn it over in your heart, and your teacher will come.

Once you set up a meeting with someone, you can begin to talk of other things: Where will you meet? How long and how often will you meet? Does the person charge or prefer an offering in exchange for services? Offerings can come in various forms instead of money: flowers, homemade breads or pastries, pottery, or something that you have to trade. Your director will also give you an idea of the kinds of things you'll be talking about, and how this practice differs from counseling or therapy. Go to the first session with questions in hand and a willing heart.

The person you meet with should also have a first-hand knowledge of spiritual practice through the centuries. Perhaps s/he will be a graduate of a Shalem program in spiritual direction, or perhaps s/he will have done private study and reading. In any event, the meeting time will include more than just talking; sometimes you and the director will actually practice meditation, or s/he will teach you a meditation to take home and try. The director will be a teacher, a friend, and a confidant, someone very special in your life.

Following Benedict's structure of work, study, and prayer, plus making a rule of life and finding a spiritual friend, are all things we can do, to come closer to life in the Spirit. These steps all help move us toward taking time, toward having time for what is good and true. Our lives will certainly change once we begin this journey. We'll experience things in a new way; what used to be important may no longer be. We'll slow down, see more, pay more attention to ourselves and others. We may even be surprised by new turns in the road.

☙ 3 ❧

Life in the Spirit

Jesus lived a life of radical insecurity. A scribe approached him one day, saying, "Teacher, I will follow you wherever you go." Jesus said to this scribe: "Foxes have holes, and birds of the air have nests; but the Son of Man has nowhere to lay his head" (Mt 8:19, 20). These are some of the saddest words in scripture, but also perhaps the most exhilarating. Listen to what else he says:

> Therefore I tell you, do not worry about your life, what you will eat or what you will drink, or about your body, what you will wear. Is not life more than food, and the body more than clothing? Look at the birds of the air; they neither sow nor reap nor gather into barns, and yet your heavenly Father feeds them. Are you not of more value than they? (Mt 6:25, 26)

He continues with yet more unorthodox thoughts:

> And can any of you by worrying add a single hour to your span of life? And why do you worry about clothing? Consider the lilies of the field, how they grow; they neither toil nor spin, yet I tell you, even Solomon in all his glory was not clothed like one of these. (Mt 6:27–29)

Jesus actually seems to have lived like this, without worry and without fear. He held on to *nothing:* owned nothing, had no home, wasn't married, didn't have kids, didn't even hold a regular job, other than following his burning passion proclaim the coming kingdom of God.

This "real Jesus" is not actually seen by many; he's been layered over, for centuries, with piety and theology. When I was a teenager, a shocking Italian film came to our small town: *The Gospel According to St. Matthew.* This Jesus was a wild-eyed prophet—wandering around, getting into trouble, always with fire in his eyes. Years later I began to read Nikos Kazantzakis's *The Last Temptation of Christ,* and this Jesus had great claws in his head as he struggled through life. The book was so intense; so unlike my own tame Jesus, I had to put it down. I couldn't imagine this radical Jesus, someone living on the edge.

Kazantzakis also wrote *Saint Francis,* with similar themes. Let me share with you Lawrence Cunningham's thoughts on the differences between simplicity and poverty, from his book *Saint Francis of Assisi:*

> Simplicity of life and poverty are not the same. There are many people who live very simple lives, either by choice or circumstance, who are not poor. Poverty does not mean simply a lack of money or goods. In its essence, poverty means radical insecurity about the basic means of life. Poverty is literally not knowing where the next meal is coming from, or the frantic fear of getting ill because there is no money for a doctor, or the gnawing despair when one recognizes the gap between the next possible time when

money will come and the actual needs of the household. It is, in short, a knowledge that the world is not solid, secure, and benign. Poverty is not only want; it is the fear and dread that derives from want. (58)

Jesus lived with this kind of poverty. Christians over the centuries—from St. Francis and his followers, to the monastics of today, to ordinary Christians—in trying to live like Jesus, have sought both simplicity of life and the greater poverty. But these somewhat romantic notions always meet up with the reality of life at some point.

Simplicity of Life

I, too, became interested in this simplicity of life, which was quite unlike what I grew up with. I grew up in the Midwest within a financially comfortable, educated family. But even coming from such a safe, stable environment, I found my life taking some interesting turns. In college and beyond I began to read Mohandas Gandhi and Martin Luther King. I followed St. Francis and St. Clare, read Albert Schweitzer and Thomas Merton, and later read Dorothy Day and Mother Teresa. I also discovered the Berrigan brothers, the Soledad brothers, Angela Davis, the Symbionese Liberation Army, and the Weathermen. This was not exactly normal reading for a small-town Ohio girl.

By the time I reached Washington, D.C., as a young woman, I was becoming radicalized. I longed to live simply; like Jesus, to understand and help the poor. I took what Jesus said to heart and earned very little, gave money away, used orange crates for dressers, and bought used cars—all to identify with people who had so very little. I still liked the nice things that my family had, but now there was no going back.

When I was ordained after six long years of training, I began working in the inner city, and saw yet another side of life: the elderly hiding away in high, lonely apartments; "street people" carrying their belongings in bags and carts; hundreds living minimally in nursing homes; beautiful prostitutes hailing down cars; and scores of people in the locked wards of St. Elizabeth's, the nation's largest hospital for the mentally ill. I visited hospitals and prisons and went out on the streets, where 10,000 shadow-people lived.

Again I thought about Jesus. It was hard to justify having money, seeing all this sorrow and heartbreak. Money should be given away. Wasn't that what Jesus did, give it all away? What was it he said to the rich man: "Go, sell what you own, give the money to the poor. . .then come, follow me" (Mk 10:21). Could he possibly have meant that? Did he really want Zacchaeus to give away half of all his possessions? Yes, I think he did. But why did he want this, what did it mean?

Perhaps Jesus meant there are things besides aggression, acquisition, and accumulation. Perhaps he meant there are people out there with nothing, and maybe you have something to give. Perhaps he also meant that to find our lives, we'll have to lose them. We'll have to empty ourselves, humble ourselves, become obedient to God. Paul speaks of such things in his letter to the Philippians:

> *Let the same mind be in you that was in Christ Jesus,*
> *who, though he was in the form*
> *of God,*
> *did not regard equality with*
> *God*
> *as something to be exploited,*
> *but emptied himself,*
> *taking the form of a slave,*
> *being born in human*
> *likeness.*
> *And being found in human*
> *form,*
> *he humbled himself*
> *and became obedient to the*
> *point of death—*
> *even death on a cross.*
> *(Phil. 2:5–8)*

This emptying is a radical notion of living, for if we begin to let go, who can tell what will happen? If we let go of possessions, or power, or people—of anything hampering our vision or keeping us from a spiritual life—what will we then see? A new direction, perhaps, some new turn in the road, something completely unexpected. Mostly, we'll begin to live with the unknown.

Living simply and letting go can be dangerous, for it means giving up. We might have to give up some of our comforts, our plans, or our relationships, or perhaps some of the unchanging picture we've formed of ourselves. Paul speaks of this new life; if anyone is in Christ, he says, s/he is a new creation: "everything old has passed away; see, everything has become new!" (2 Cor 5:17) He also speaks of early Christians and their trials:

> We are treated as impostors, and yet are true; as unknown, and yet are well known; as dying, and see—we are alive; as punished, and yet not killed; as sorrowful, yet always rejoicing; as poor, yet making many rich; as having nothing, and yet possessing everything. (2 Cor 6:8–10)

And in the "having nothing" we come to something else altogether: radical insecurity. Yet even in this insecurity, Paul says we possess everything.

Radical Insecurity

Now listen to these words of Janice Deaner, from her strange and moving novel *The Body Spoken*. In this story a woman and a man, strangers, get on a train and go across country. The woman has lived as a man for the past several years. In a series of flashbacks, she tells the stranger her life story. At one point in the past, she had worked with a group of old people—washing them, cleaning them, and helping them through their sorrow:

> So I sat down next to Leopold Harry on the wooden seat in the marble shower and he closed his eyes and watched

his breath and listened. It began to fascinate me, the power of grace, the core that lay deep down inside someone, that when touched, sent things up, answers, strengths, occurrences, as if power dwelled down there. There seemed to be nothing else in the face of a life that could take your family, your legs, your spine, your lover, strip you of everything, make loss the only thing you knew. (269)

I understand this loss that Deaner talks about, so huge that nothing is left. And I understand the "power of grace" and the radical insecurity that sometimes precedes it. In a period of a few years, perhaps like some of you, I lost everything I had to lose during a shattering divorce: I lost my home; my children; my gardens, animals, and plants; my job; and my marriage. For a long time, radical insecurity became an everyday nightmare reality, until I was able to find the power of grace.

After years of unhappiness in a difficult marriage, I one day found myself separated from my spouse and locked out of my home in Virginia. I had nowhere to turn, had been visiting in another state, and had no funds for legal representation. Besides having no home and no way to keep my job, I was also worn to the bone and needed to rest. I grew thin and frail, tried to survive one day and then the next. This was the beginning of the "fear and dread" that Cunningham talks about, the real poverty of living.

I was finally able to return to Virginia, but for two years I wandered from place to place, living with friends and strangers. I lived in dark basements, farmhouses, living rooms of students, attics, and more dark basements. I came to know firsthand, radical insecurity, radical trust, and the surprise of grace. I often couldn't see my way. But when I couldn't pray, others prayed for me; when I couldn't see any light at all, others held up their lamps. When I thought I had no one to talk to, someone would suddenly appear.

Jesus was no stranger to this kind of radical insecurity. There were days when he had no food, no shelter, and no clear direction. But he trusted God to guide him: he seemed to live completely by grace, and this grace sustained him. The love holding him up flowed like a river around him, and he would go on to find his way, with the help of many friends. Life in the Spirit is like this—not always knowing or understanding, but trusting in what's to come.

Contrary to what some believe, Jesus didn't have an easy road map. He didn't always know what would happen next or what his fate would be. But during his final days, he got down on his knees in a garden and prayed. He prayed to be released, he prayed for guidance, and he prayed for protection: he couldn't see the series of events about to unfold, but he prayed not to die. "Your will be done," he said at last, and then he got up and carried on.

Carrying on is the hard part when we can't see the events in front of us. We rub our crystal balls and try to read the tea leaves, but in the end we just don't know what's coming. And it's that not knowing that makes life so difficult. But sometimes we have a glimpse of things: we feel a quiet touch or sense a presence. Sometimes we know, without a doubt, that we're cared for at a deep level. When the way becomes clearer, what we see is that we're carried through our troubles, lifted up by the surprising power of grace.

The Power of Grace

Living simply in the midst of sorrow and learning to live with radical insecurity can bring us to the edge of *grace*—that well of deep peace that abides no matter the situation, no matter the time, no matter the place. "Abide in me," Jesus says, "as I abide in you. . . .I am the vine, you are the branches. Those who abide in me and I in them bear much fruit." (Jn 15:4, 5) *Abide* is such a wonderful word, from the Latin *meno*, meaning "to remain, continue." But even more wonderful is grace.

"What is this grace that you Christians talk about?" someone asked. A Shalem group was gathered for morning meditation, at the Paulist House near Catholic University. We met downstairs. The large room held silence and overlooked a grassy yard; morning light came through the windows. The group was a mix of many people from within and outside the church.

What is this grace? The gospel of John tells us: "And the Word became flesh and lived among us, and we have seen his glory, the glory as of a father's only son, full of grace and truth" (1:14). John also proclaims, "From his fullness we have all received, grace upon grace" (1:16). This is the grace that stayed in the desert with Jesus when "angels came and waited on him" (Mt 4:11); the grace of the women—Mary, Joanna, Susanna—who provided for Jesus and others "out of their resources" (Lk 8:2); the grace Jesus received at the Mount of Olives, when he asked that his "cup" be removed: "Then an angel from heaven appeared to him and gave him strength" (Lk 22:43); the grace given to the three Marys as they stood at the foot of the cross (Jn 19:25). Unexpected strength, unexpected provision, unexpected care: all these things are grace.

Jesus' life was a life of grace. It bore and sustained him through the worst of trials— through days of no food, no clothing, and nowhere to live. He preached that necessary things would be supplied: "But strive first for the kingdom of God and his righteousness, and all these things will be given to you as well" (Mt 6:33). "Don't worry about tomorrow," he said, "for tomorrow will bring worries of its own. Today's trouble is enough for today" (Mt 6:34).

Jesus lived in present time. The past didn't seem to be part of his life, and the present was concerned with the kingdom of God. "None of you can become my disciple if you do not give up all your possessions" (Lk 14:33). He sent his disciples out to "every town and place where he himself intended to go," telling them to carry no purse, no bag, and no extra sandals. The disciples were dependent on grace for what they wore, what they ate, and where they stayed. If they were received and heard, Jesus bid them say: "The kingdom of God has come near to you" (Lk 10:1–9).

Grace also comes to us, in present time. In my own experience, many gifts came during a difficult time: gifts of money, friendship, shelter, and comfort. God's grace lives in abundance, but we don't always see it. When we do, grace seems to grow as we live in the present and begin to experience deep peace. Grace is with us when we wake and when we go to sleep. It comes in the form of angels, in strangers on a bus or plane, in kind words of children, in surprising gifts, and in the steady love of family and friends. Grace comes to us in Jesus. "For he is our peace," says Ephesians 2:14:

> So he came and proclaimed peace to you who were far off and peace to those who were near. . . .So then you are no longer strangers and aliens, but you are citizens with the saints and also members of the household of God. (Eph 2:17, 19)

We can learn to watch for this grace, to be aware of it every day. As our lives slow down through the use of prayer, we begin to see small moments of grace in any given day. They slip in and out like fireflies in July, blinking at us, letting us know we're cared for, watched over, and loved. But mostly these moments pass us by: we miss them as they happen, for we're in too much of a hurry to see them. Slowing down and winding down, like anything else, takes time and practice. Let's take a look now at some notions of rest.

✤ 4 ✤

Sabbath Time

So we return to living a day at a time, with the grace given to us, as Jesus himself lived. But how do we find our "Sabbath time," that time of rest and peace? Margaret Guenther, in *The Practice of Prayer*, says if we can't manage twenty-four hours, we can at least make the habit of "building little sabbaths into our crowded days" (153). It's easier to study the saints and read about meditation than to actually do it. Setting aside quiet time is not easy, and may prove to be quite difficult. Says Guenther:

> Letting ourselves rest in silence is the ultimate simplification and, at the same time, is the most difficult kind of prayer for many of us. (*Practice*, 155)

The Portable Sabbath

Years ago I read an article in *The Washington Post*, that made some things fall in place for me. The article was "The Portable Sabbath: Why Americans Have Turned to Meditation" by Harvey Cox, from his book *Turning East*. He says that for Christians and Jews, meditation fills the needs once filled by the Jewish Sabbath—that quiet time from sundown Friday to sundown Saturday when no work was done. Sabbath was the day of rest, the final day of creation. In fact, when Genesis tells us that God "rested" on the seventh day, *rest* is a rare Hebrew verb meaning "to draw one's breath." God literally drew breath and rested, after all the work was done.

Cox says we can no longer return to the slower time of our ancestors; our lives are too harried, too hurried, too fast.

> Can we ever regain the glorious vision of Sabbath as a radiant queen, a jeweled sovereign who comes to visit, bringing warmth and joy in her train? The poor and often inept Hasidic Jews in the stories of Isaac Bashevis Singer may bicker and complain, and they surely suffer, but when the sun goes down and the lamps begin to flicker on Friday evening, a kind of magic touches their world. (*Sabbath*)

That magic is gone from us now, and we have to find our own. And for many, the church no longer offers a silence that sustains. Sunday morning is a traditional time of gathering, of celebrating the Eucharist and ancient liturgy, of listening to revered scriptures, but it's not usually a time of rest. I've talked with any number of older people who are simply worn out with the doctrine, liturgy, and work of the church; they're now looking for rest and peace. For the most part, they find this rest in silence and meditation.

This is not to say that silence can take the place of the bread and wine of Jesus, but we have lost something vital and necessary in our worship. So our Sabbath time becomes movable, portable, as we find small parts of it during a day, carry it with us through a week, or practice it with a group in meditation. The "seventh day" is now pieces of days when we do nothing, see no one, go nowhere. In Jewish thought, this is Yahweh's time:

> The seventh day is to Yahweh, and one keeps it holy not by doing things for God or even for one's fellow human beings. One keeps it holy by doing nothing. (*Sabbath*)

Right now we need to find this time—to carve it out in bits and pieces from our daily lives and work. We need to look once again at how and where we spend our time. Perhaps we need to actually map it out: how many hours for *work*? How many for *children, family, friends*? How many hours for *exercise* and *relaxation*: TV, videos, magazines, books? How many hours for *chores* and *homework*: laundry, dishes, cleaning, cooking, mowing, repairs; plus our gardens, our plants and animals?

Now factor in time for prayer and quiet. Where can it fit; how can it find a niche? What can be eliminated that's unnecessary, or what can be consolidated? Think of all those little trips in any one day: the post office, grocery store, drugstore, library, shopping at the mall. Perhaps nothing can be reworked or consolidated in an already busy day. Perhaps only an iron will can change the pattern of our times, or a spirit ready for change.

Finding time is possible, though. My late beloved bishop, John Thomas Walker, got up every morning at 5:00 AM to say his prayers, read his books, and meditate. He didn't boast of this, but said that before the day began it was his only time to be alone. John's good friend, Archbishop Desmond Tutu of South Africa, still keeps the same practice of getting up early in the morning to attend to prayer. The lights of both these men have shone brightly in our world for justice and peace. And their work in the world, like Jesus', has come from the depths of silence.

Mindfulness Day

Thich Nhat Hanh, in *The Miracle of Mindfulness*, has given us another model: setting a day aside each week to be "mindful." He suggests Saturday, but any day will do—whatever works with your schedule. Those of you with young children and teenagers will have a harder time arranging this, but it's not impossible. On whatever day you choose, Nhat Hanh advises you to "forget the work you do during the other days" (87). Let's imagine this weekday or Saturday, according to Nhat Hanh's suggestions, as well as a few of my own.

Morning. When you wake, remind yourself that this is your time. There's no place to go, nothing to do. No friends are arriving, and you have no meetings. You have also turned off the telephone. Relax in bed and feel a smile on your face. *Breathe*: breathe in, breathe out, just breathe. Rise slowly from your bed—no rush— and take care of morning ablutions: brush your teeth, wash your face. Take a half-hour bath, soaking in the tub, or take a refreshing shower. Maintain a half-smile; do everything slowly and mindfully.

Before getting started on a few morning chores, take a nice half-hour walk. But first, feed all your animals and let them out to stretch. You can stretch with them as well. Then begin your neighborhood walk, no rush, saying a few prayers or reciting psalms as you go along. Breathe again and let yourself relax. After the walk, do a few chores carefully and mindfully: washing dishes, dusting, making beds. "Don't do any task in order to get it over with. . . .Enjoy and be one with your work" (*Miracle,* 29).

Hold to your silence as best you can. There's no need to talk on the phone, or even to talk with others present. If you have morning time left over after the bath, the walk, the chores, do a little reading or writing: a favorite book, some scripture, a handwritten note to a friend. "While reading the sacred text, know what you are reading; while writing the letter, know what you are writing" (*Miracle,* 88). Prepare yourself a cup of tea; allow your mind to be bright and clear. Relax and breathe, and enjoy your morning.

Afternoon. Perhaps you have had a small breakfast—an apple, a piece of cheese, some toast or bread—and now it's time to fix yourself some lunch. Choose simple foods: soup, salad, or bread again, some fresh fruit. Take time to meditate on the food: its color and shape, its content. Eat in silence; there's no need for radio, CDs, or

TV. Just pay attention to your food and enjoy it. Give thanks for the food, and for this day.

After the meal, take some time to work outside. Do a little planting, a little digging, some work in the garden—work with your hands. Watch clouds, look at trees in the sunlight, gather flowers, go for another walk. There's no place to go, no one to be, nothing to do. "This is the day that the Lord has made; let us rejoice and be glad in it" (Ps 118:24). Following your outside time, make another cup or pot of tea. Says Nhat Hanh:

> Don't drink your tea like someone who gulps down a cup of coffee during a workbreak. Drink your tea slowly and reverently, as if it is the axis on which the whole earth revolves—slowly, evenly, without rushing toward the future. Live the actual moment. Only this actual moment is life. (*Miracle*, 30)

Stay in present time, relax and breathe, and enjoy your afternoon.

Evening. If you haven't already, read some scripture, find a good book, write letters to friends. Stay away from noise, distractions, and bad news: there's no need for email, cell phones, television, or even the newspaper on your quiet day. Stay in present time. Don't think ahead about the things you have to do. Don't think behind. Just enjoy your evening, as the light begins to fade away.

Spend time with your animals. Feed them, brush their coats, let them know you love them. Scratch their ears and backs. Then eat lightly, so as not to weigh yourself down. Eat some fruit, drink some juice or water, have a little salad, cook a few vegetables. If you didn't take time in the afternoon for your walk, "take a slow walk in the fresh night air" (*Miracle*, 30). Say some prayers for those you love; say some prayers for yourself. Breathe in the air and relax.

Now it's time to rest. Before going to sleep, sit in meditation for a half-hour or an hour. Or alternate your walking and your sitting: twenty minutes slow walking, twenty minutes sitting, twenty minutes slow walking. Follow your breath, watch your steps, be grateful for the day. Finally, go to your room, prepare for bed, and go to sleep, keeping the same mindfulness you have kept throughout the day. *No place to go, nothing to do, just sleep.*

Nhat Hanh says we must find a way to allow ourselves a day of mindfulness; this day will have an "immeasurable effect" on the other days of the week:

> After only three months of observing such a day of mindfulness once a week, I know that you will see a significant change in your life. The day of mindfulness will begin to penetrate the other days of the week, enabling you to eventually live seven days a week in mindfulness. (*Miracle,* 31)

Treasure and Pearls

We've thought about Sabbath time, we've thought about a day of mindfulness, now let's look at some of Jesus' parables once again. Look at Matthew 13, for instance, where we have a group of picture parables: the mustard seed (31–32), the yeast in the flour (33), the treasure hidden in a field (44), the pearl of great value (45–46). What do these all have in common? These small parables all talk about the same thing, the kingdom of heaven. Jesus says, "The kingdom of heaven is like" a seed, yeast, a treasure, a pearl.

Matthew doesn't refer to "heaven" as something in another time. On the contrary, he's talking about the present. Jesus is saying: The kingdom is here, right now in your midst.

The kingdom of heaven is small, like a mustard seed, but the seed can grow to the size of a shrub or tree—so high that birds fly in and make nests in its branches. The yeast in the flour is even smaller than the seed, but as it spreads, it creates a round loaf to place in an oven.

The treasure in the field is a bit different: It's not small or growing, it's hidden. Someone finds it, waiting just beneath the surface in a field or garden. The person who finds it is so happy, so joyful, that he reburies the treasure, sells *everything* to buy the field.

Finally is the merchant searching the whole of the world for the most beautiful pearls. One day, he finds one of particularly "great value." Like the person who purchased an entire field for a single treasure, he sells all that he has to buy it.

These are touching stories, and Jesus' point is clear: Look around you, he says, be aware. The kingdom is growing where you work, where you eat, and where you sleep. You may not see it; it may be too small or too hidden away—waiting under the earth, or sitting on a seller's table. But when you do see it, you'll know great joy. Nothing else will matter. You'll give away all that you have to own this treasure or this pearl.

This is the message we have in these small stories: Be awake! Be alive! Look around! The "kingdom of heaven" is in front of you! Jesus is telling us to wake up and see what's before us. These stories are not for told entertainment, but to teach listeners to focus, to see clearly. Jesus tells them so that people will think about, pay attention to, God's kingdom in their midst.

During any given day, you and I focus—on what? Our hair, our clothes, our tasks at work; our relationships, food, chores, meetings. Do this, do that, get it done. We forget to look at the treasure hidden in the field. We forget to search for, the iridescent pearl shining on a table. We're busy, we're tired, we're sad, we're angry: we don't have time. But *there it is*, Jesus says, all around you, and you're missing it everyday.

Of all the creatures and creations in Matthew 13's parables—seeds, sowers, birds, nests, shrubs; yeast, flour, a treasure in a field, a merchant, a pearl—I like the merchant best. The tiny story tells us he's searching for fine pearls. The merchant is on a quest, making a journey. I see him sailing, and I see him looking in markets and bazaars. He's focused, he's searching, he's trying to find one fine pearl. And when he finds it, he sells everything away—all that he has.

Jesus' message is radical. Perhaps we'll never match the intensity of what he asks his listeners to do. We don't live in first century Palestine, and most of us aren't watching for the end of the world. But we can try to find peace in small glimpses as we hurry through our days. We can pause when we hear bells. We can stop to say a prayer. We can slow down to breathe, to be alive. We can look for the kingdom of heaven, as it grows and shines around us.

✒ 5 ✒

Practicing Peace

We've now taken a look at several practices in Christian living: *the rhythm of hours, making a rule, life in the Spirit, Sabbath time.* Now comes the most difficult of all—*practicing peace.* Peace is sometimes easy to talk, or write about, but not so easy to live. Learning to create peace, make peace, *wage* peace, can be a lifelong, lonely task. But Jesus gives us a promise:

> But the Advocate, the Holy Spirit, whom the Father will send in my name, will teach you everything, and remind you of all that I have said to you. Peace I leave with you; my peace I give to you. I do not give to you as the world gives. Do not let your hearts be troubled, and do not let them be afraid. (Jn 14:26, 27)

My peace I give to you, he says. But what is this peace? The letter to the Philippians says: "And the peace of God, which surpasses all understanding, will guard your hearts and your minds in Christ Jesus" (4:7). After the terror of September 11, 2001, I had to sort this through, figure out what this peace meant. Here again is Jesus speaking, from Matthew 5:43–46:

> You have heard that it was said, 'You shall love your neighbor and hate your enemy.' But I say to you, Love your enemies and pray for those who persecute you, so that you may be children of your Father in heaven; for he makes his sun rise on the evil and on the good, and sends rain on the righteous and on the unrighteous. For if you love those who love you, what reward do you have?

Especially after the fall of the World Trade Center Towers, the destruction of the Pentagon and the crater in a Pennsylvania field, I didn't understand these words. How could Jesus say these things? "You have heard that it was said, an 'eye for an eye and a tooth for a tooth.' But I say to you, Do not resist an evildoer" (Mt 5:38, 39). But I could understand the rescue workers removing megatons of metal and steel and glass, one bucketful at a time. The picture was all too huge, I could make sense of just one bucketful—a small fragment of peace, from which I tried to get back to the whole.

I think of peace this way now. I take it in small doses, practice it in parts. I think of all creation—animals, plants, and people—finding their way to peace. I try to stay in the reality of one day, and to do what I can in that day to carry my small bucketful. Let's take a look now at some parts of practicing peace, as possibilities for our lives: *reverence for life, generosity, good health, and reconciliation.* Each of these is a large bucketful.

Reverence for life

As a child, I was greatly influenced by my mother, who wouldn't let me kill butterflies or any other living thing. As a young adult, I came under the influence of Albert Schweitzer's "reverence for life" philosophy. Schweitzer—pastor, musician, and medical missionary—founded a hospital in French Equatorial Africa. At the hospital, plants and animals were not harmed; even bees and flies went unharmed. Says Erica Anderson, in her book *The Schweitzer Album*:

> No bird or animal in the hospital village—hen or pig or sheep—is killed for food. Fish and crocodile meat brought by fishermen are occasionally served at table, but Schweitzer himself in recent years has given up eating either meat or fish, even the liver dumplings he used to relish and enjoy. 'I can't eat anything that was alive any more.' When a man questioned him on his philosophy and said that God made fish and fowl for people to eat, he answered, 'Not at all. Only when a creature can't exist without feeding on other animals may it be fed so.' (*Schweitzer*, 38)

Besides caring for thousands of patients, the doctor also cared for wild pigs, chickens, goats, cats, antelopes, pelicans, chimps, parrots, gorillas. Schweitzer created both a hospital village and a leper village in Lambarene. For his work there and for his philosophy, he won the Nobel Prize for Peace in 1952. "A Christian is one who has the spirit of Christ," he said. "This is the only theology." This spirit of Christ, I believe, includes a reverence for all creation: our animals, our plants, and our children.

Animals. Through the influence of my mother and Schweitzer, I had stopped eating animals by my twenties. I stopped in stages: first giving up beef and pork, then chicken and turkey, then fish and seafood. Like Schweitzer, I opposed animal experimentation and exploitation, whether in labs, circuses, or zoos. The last time I visited the Washington National Zoo, in the 1970s, I saw great elephants heavily chained together only a few feet apart; after that I never returned.
I also began to read articles on animal abuse and inhumane conditions in the United States. Rich Heffern, in "The Ethics of Eating" in the *National Catholic Reporter*, says this about pigs:

> Pigs are intelligent, sensitive and clean animals. But those unfortunate enough to be born on a large factory farm face a life of confinement and cruelty, according to the Humane Farming Association. After impregnation, a factory farm sow is locked in a narrow metal gestation crate, 24 inches wide and long enough so that she can move forward and backward only a few inches. By conveyer belt, she is fed at one end of the crate and her feces collected at the other.

Heffern says that, deprived of all exercise, the sow lives in a constant state of distress, "frantically and repeatedly" biting her metal bars. The Humane Farming Association calls these "desolate pig prisons." After the sow gives birth, the piglets are separated from her; the sow is impregnated again and sent back to the crate. The cycle is repeated until she is finally sent to slaughter ("Ethics," 7).
Now listen to the beauty of Galway Kinnell's *St. Francis and the Sow:*

The bud
stands for all things,
even for those things that don't flower,
for everything flowers, from within, of self-blessing;
though sometimes it is necessary
to reteach a thing its loveliness,
to put a hand on its brow
of the flower
and retell it in words and in touch
it is lovely
until it flowers again from within, of self-blessing;
as Saint Francis
put his hand on the creased forehead
of the sow, and told her in words and in touch
blessings of earth on the sow, and the sow
began remembering all down her thick length,
from the earthen snout all the way
through the fodder and slops to the spiritual curl of the tail,
from the hard spininess spiked out from the spine
down through the great broken heart
to the sheer blue milken dreaminess spurting and
shuddering
from the fourteen teats into the fourteen mouths sucking
and blowing beneath them:
the long, perfect loveliness of sow.

Let that poem sink in. Savor it: the loveliness of the sow, the hand on her head, her babies drinking milk. This is a completely different view of a sow, and of the life she leads on earth. Her life can be as precious, and as revered, as our own. But we don't have just pigs on the planet: we also have chickens and turkeys, cows and calves, sheep, horses, and deer—all deserving life.

Plants. Who is there to speak for our animals? And who will speak for our plants and trees? Two summers ago the university in my town cleared land for new tennis courts, just down from my driveway. The night before the destruction began, some of us went over to see the house on the property and the trees: large furs and pines, cherries, maples, big oaks, plus rosebushes and tiger lilies and patches of summer flowers. The next day large tractors and destroying machines came, and they stayed months—sawing, dragging, buzzing, breaking. Nothing at all was spared.

Yet Schweitzer, deep in Africa, rerouted an entire driveway leading to his hospital, so one large tree could be saved. He didn't harm the flowering plants, and didn't harm the trees. Jane Goodall and Marc Bekoff speak to this in *The Ten Trusts:*

> We show, in the Eighth Trust ["Have the Courage of Our Convictions"], that by steadfastly voicing our concerns, upholding our beliefs, and taking action, we can bring about change. Once a sufficient number of people take action, we can make changes that benefit all animals and the Earth. (120)

Children. Who will speak for our animals, our plants, and our children? I once worked as a chaplain for a women's hospital in Washington, D.C. Live births and abortions balanced out: approximately 2,500 each, per year. Of the thousands of women I spoke with, only a handful had chosen abortion for medical reasons. The rest felt it *just wasn't the right time* to have a child. A few doctors also performed late-term abortions; the fetus was aborted with saline solution, causing burning and suffocation. Nurses told me that babies were sometimes born alive, then left to die.

Talking with the women over the years and seeing abortion firsthand changed my views; I became a strong advocate for adoption. Children were available all over the world, I learned, from Korea, China, South America, India, Eastern Europe, and within the United States. The process took time and money, but it was a great gift in the end. I myself adopted two children from Korea, and presented "adoption as an option" to families at the hospital where I worked.

Reverence for life is *mercy*, at the deepest part of the well. This reverence is also compassion—loving-kindness for plants, for animals, and for children. Taking care of these, revering these, is part of our peacemaking practice. Jesus says: "Blessed are the merciful, for they will receive mercy. Blessed are the pure in heart, for they will see God. Blessed are the peacemakers, for they will be called children of God" (Mt 5: 7–9)

Generosity

Besides reverence for life, another part of peace is a glad and willing heart. As Luke says: "give and it will be given to you. A good measure, pressed down, shaken together, running over, will be put into your lap" (6:38). This theme of giving runs throughout the Hebrew and New Testament scriptures. The question for us is: what do we have that we can give away? Probably much more than we realize. At the least, we have *money, abundance,* and *time.*

Money. Tithe simply means tenth, giving ten percent of your income, or your land's produce away. Deuteronomy 14:22 tells us of a "tenth" offering: "Set apart a tithe of all the yield of your seed that is brought in yearly from the field." This produce was offered yearly at the harvest festival (Deut 16:9–12); every third year the tithe went to Levites, resident aliens, orphans, and widows of the towns of Israel (Deut 14: 28, 29). Tithing people would be blessed:

> Look down from your holy habitation, from heaven, and
> bless your people Israel and the ground that you have given
> us, as you swore to your ancestors—a land flowing with
> milk and honey. (Deut 26:15)

We can give money, if nothing else, to the Red Cross, to Oxfam, to UNICEF, to Episcopal Relief and Development, to Amnesty International. We can fund Tree of Life Imports for craftspeople in South America, or Heifer International, giving gifts of animals and seedlings to families around the world. We can give to Habitat for Humanity, the Salvation Army, People for the Ethical Treatment of Animals (PETA), or the Animal Protection Institute (API). "Send out your bread upon the waters," says Ecclesiastes, "for after many days you will get it back" (11:1).

Abundance. We should also give of our abundance, whatever it may be. The books of Moses again give us guidelines. Moses, in Leviticus, calls the congregation of Israel to holiness:

> You shall be holy, for I the Lord your God am holy. . . .When you reap the harvest of your land, you shall not reap to the very edges of your field, or the gather gleanings of your harvest. You shall not strip your vineyard bare, or gather the fallen grapes of your vineyard; you shall leave them for the poor and the alien: I am the Lord your God. (19:2, 9, 10)

The poor and aliens were once again cared for by the House of Israel: no one went without, not even strangers in the midst of the tribal clans.

Most of us like to keep the harvest for ourselves; we don't like to share our grapes. But perhaps we do indeed have an excess of food from what we've grown, or an excess of clothing sitting in piles. Think about the things that you own: What do you have in abundance? Cars, clothing, food, computers, televisions, gadgets, toys? What of all these could you share? Another passage in Leviticus entreats the people of Israel to the highest commandment: "you shall love your neighbor as yourself" (19:18).

Time. We also have time to give away, even though our days are always fast. We watch our watches and clocks; run our lives against both. How long has it been since you stopped to listen? Since you really slowed down to hear what someone had to say—your spouse, or child, your mother or father, maybe one or another of your friends? How long has it been since you gave your time? By Ladling soup in a soup line, sitting in a dugout to coach kids, or driving to a person's house to teach her to read? Matthew says: "You received without payment; give without payment" (10:8).

Years ago, in Arlington, Virginia, I tutored Kim from Vietnam.

Kim's house was always full, with an entire camp of people: children, aunts, uncles, husband, cousins. I ended up tutoring many of them. But one day I arrived to find a deserted house. The family had moved, and I didn't know how to find them. A few weeks later I was walking down a grocery aisle and heard a voice: *Teacher! Teacher!* Kim, a tiny boat woman, ran toward me in tears with arms outstretched. We embraced in the aisle, and my joy equaled hers. The letter of James tells us:

> Every generous act of giving, with every perfect gift, is from above, coming down from the Father of lights, with whom there is no variation or shadow due to change. (Jas 1:17)

Kim and her family had given me much more than I could ever give them. That one day alone was
a gift of a lifetime.

Good Health

Reverence for life, generosity, good health: all are parts of practicing peace. And good health extends beyond diet and physical fitness: it has to do with ridding violence from our lives and working hard to overcome addiction to drugs, sex, alcohol, nicotine, caffeine, food—to anything that disturbs the peaceful, natural state of our minds. Thich Nhat Hanh writes in *Touching Peace*:

> Aware of the suffering caused by unmindful consumption, I am committed to cultivating good health, both physical and mental, for myself, my family, and my society by practicing mindful eating, drinking, and consuming. I will ingest only items that preserve peace, well-being, and joy in my body, in my consciousness, and in the collective body and consciousness of my family and society. (89)

Let's consider for a moment, some of the great hindrances to good health in our lives: alcohol and drugs; TV, film, and videos; eating habits and sexual practice.

Alcohol and drugs. I was fortunate, growing up, to come under the influence of my paternal grandmother. Laila cared for plants and also had a great knowledge of health. My grandmother was a licensed massage therapist; she taught me the names of bones and organs of the body. Laila counseled me to avoid three things—coffee, caffeine tea, and alcohol. Her own mother had been a strong temperance woman who passed her beliefs down the family line. To this day I avoid stimulants and have always enjoyed being a teetotaler.

But I've seen up close friends, relatives, and students who used alcohol and drugs, and the devastating effects their addiction caused not only to the users, but to the wider circle of their friends and families. This world of drugs and alcohol causes a great deal of suffering, but it's possible to find help and relief through such groups of Alcoholics Anonymous (AA), Narcotics Anonymous (NA), and Alanon. We can learn to take a stand:

> The fruit and grain that produce alcoholic beverages use farmland that could be producing food for those who are hungry. . . .To stop drinking is a statement to our children and our society that this is a substance not worthy of our support. . . .In persuading one person to refrain from drinking, we make the world a safer place. (*Touching,* 92)

TV, film, and videos. Besides violence done to ourselves with alcohol and drugs, we surround ourselves with violent television, film, and videos. Long ago I stopped watching television for about fifteen years. When I returned to it, everything on the screen seemed very fast and violent. I lost sleep at night: my mind would replay, in detail, all the scenes I'd seen. I couldn't rest, couldn't relax, and violent images filled my mind. Then I started to get used to it.

> When we watch TV, read magazines or books, or pick up the telephone, we only make our condition worse if our condition is not mindful. During one hour watching a film filled with violence, we water the seeds of violence, hatred, and fear in us. We do that, and we let our children do that.

We need to have family meetings to discuss an intelligent policy for television watching. (*Touching,* 93)

My university students—over 3,000 now—love action and violence in films; this is what they're used to, what they know. They've grown up watching hours of MTV weekly and playing violent video games. They're bored if a film or game is too slow. Unhooking our children, friends, and families from this kind of everyday violence may be our greatest task. Teaching them to slow down and notice, just teaching them to breathe, can be lifelong work. Our peace education begins at home, where it will be a daily, difficult, and necessary task.

Eating habits and sexual practice. Paul tells us that we are God's temple and that God's Spirit dwells in us (1 Cor 3:16). But we don't think of our bodies in this way. Our food consumption can easily go out of control, and national news tells us sixty percent of Americans are overweight. We take food and toxins into our bodies, causing more damage. With a little practice, we can eliminate harmful things from our diet: sugar, daily sodas and caffeine, animal fat and hormones. We can begin to eat simply again, finding peace in the joys of beautiful fruits and vegetables, wholesome breads, and clear, natural water.

And just as we exploit our "temples" with food, we misuse them sexually. We find partners, trade partners, and change partners, rather than experiencing love and long-term commitment. But the truth of the matter is that we can find peace within ourselves, and that it is not always necessary to have a partner or to remarry. We have inside us our own hermitage, and can begin to think of our bodies as places where the Spirit dwells.

> You yourself are sufficient. When you transform yourself into a comfortable hermitage, with air, light, and order inside, you begin to feel peace, joy, and happiness, and you begin to be someone others can rely on. Your child. . . brothers and sisters can all rely on you. (*Touching,* 109)

Reconciliation

And now we come to *reconciliation*, the hardest part: creating peace with our families, friends, co-workers, and neighbors. Most of us live in conflict of one kind or another; we fight with our parents, cousins, husbands or wives, significant others, people in the work-place—the list goes on. This is our everyday life. But our scriptures give us some wisdom:

> Be angry but do not sin; do not let the sun go down on your anger, and do not make room for the devil. . . .Put away from you all bitterness and wrath and anger and wrangling and slander, together with all malice, and be kind to one another, tenderhearted, forgiving one another, as God in Christ has forgiven you. (Eph 4:26, 27, 31, 32)

The key word here is *forgiving*. In the gospel of Matthew, Peter comes to Jesus and asks how many times he should forgive if he is sinned against. Jesus tells him "Not seven times, but. . .seventy-seven times" (18:21, 22). Matthew also shows Jesus discussing the problem of bringing a gift to an altar, then remembering that a conflict still exists with a brother or sister. First be reconciled, says Jesus, "then come and offer your gift" (5:23, 24).

Besides our own Christian scriptures, I have found the "Peace Treaty" chapter in Nhat Hanh's *Touching Peace* to be most helpful. This is a practical, everyday method including basics of not sup-pressing anger, breathing and apologizing, meeting and listening.

Not suppressing anger. What do most of us do with anger? We stuff it, deep down inside. Or we let it erupt, harming others around us. Neither way is helpful. The stuffing method can be extremely dam-aging, with long-lasting results. Nhat Hanh recommends a time limit:

> We have up to twenty-four hours to calm ourselves. Then we must tell the other person we are angry. We do not have the right to keep our anger any longer than that. If we do, it becomes poisonous, and it may destroy us and the person we love. (65)

He suggests writing a "Peace Note" that tells the person you're angry and asks for a meeting. Before the meeting happens, we should hold a "moratorium" on speech and actions, refraining from doing anything else that might cause further damage.

Breathing and apologizing. After the Peace Note has been delivered, by hand or by mail, it's time for both sides to breathe and be mindful. Most of us don't do anything like this; instead we escalate, dropping even bigger bombs on each other. We line up our friends, tell them the story, and list our grievances. We blame the other person. Instead, we should breathe slowly as we walk or sit, looking deeply to see how our actions have caused suffering or harm.

After we have practiced sitting, walking, breathing, and looking deep within, then is a good time to apologize. It doesn't matter who's right or wrong, and we don't need to wait until the meeting. A quick email, note or call—anything will do. As soon as we realize our error, we should say "I'm sorry for the hurt" and not make an attempt to justify ourselves. The apology alone will do wonders to relieve the other person's suffering.

Meeting/listening. As Nhat Hanh says: "Deep listening is the basis for reconciliation" (88). He suggests meeting on a Friday evening: "Friday evening is a good time to defuse all the bombs, big or small, so that we will have the whole weekend for our enjoyment" (66). Whatever the day of meeting, it should be when we're ready. If the other person is still not calm, and the twenty-four hours have passed by, then perhaps extra time is needed.

Once both parties agree to meet, then it's time for listening. This should be without prejudice, without judging or reacting—just deep listening. Each party should sit and actively work order to understand the other. The goal is not to defend or justify, but to listen "so attentively that we will be able to hear what the other person is saying, and also what is being left unsaid" (88). In doing this, the pain and suffering on both sides will lessen and begin to heal.

Reconciliation is hard work. Simple forgiveness is one thing: being able to forgive, forget, and let go, possibly without even seeing the person again. Reconciliation is something else altogether, and includes starting over again. It would be so much easier just to complain or to blame. But listen to what the letter of James has to say: it speaks of "the tongue," which makes many mistakes:

> Or look at ships: though they are so large that it takes strong winds to drive them, yet they are guided by a very small rudder wherever the will of the pilot directs. So also the tongue is a small member, yet it boasts of great exploits. How great a forest is set ablaze by a small fire! And the tongue is a fire. (Jas 3:4–6)

Watching our tongues and opening our hearts will give us a deeper peace. This peace will move out slowly, like ripples on a beautiful pond—beyond ourselves, into a greater lake or sea.

As twenty-first century Christians, we're called to practice peace and make peace in a world far from healing. We can do this through *reverence for life*, through *generosity* and *good health*, through acts of *forgiveness* and *reconciliation*. None of this is easy; it all takes practice and time. But if we begin these practices, then we'll start to heal from past hurts and grievances, from all harmful things. If we begin to heal, then others around us will begin to heal and, find peace themselves.

> But the wisdom from above is first pure, then peaceable, gentle, willing to yield, full of mercy and good fruits, without a trace of partiality or hypocrisy. And a harvest of righteousness is sown in peace for those who make peace. (Jas 3:17, 18)

Let me tell you a final story, from my inner city days. Reggie and I had met in meditation classes at our parish. One day Reg beat someone badly, and afterwards I went to visit him in jail. He was shaky and confused, living in solitary confinement, but he told me the breathing meditations helped. We talked through a thick glass wall, with telephones on either side. Then a loud buzzer sounded and our conversation cut off. We were left staring at each other, unable to speak. Reggie stood and put his black hand on the glass wall;

I stood and put my white hand over his. We stood this way for a time, then he smiled and was gone. In one quiet moment, in a lonely place, Reg and I found the "peace that passes all understanding."

This is the *Peace of the Lord*, and it waits for us in the jails and prisons of our lives until we can make the final trip to become children of light. Our healing stories, healing prayer, and healing practice all lead us in this direction. Paul tells us to be "imitators of God," to live in love:

> For once you were darkness, but now in the Lord you are light. Live as children of the light—for the fruit of the light is found in all that is good and right and true. Try to find out what is pleasing to the Lord. (Eph 5: 8–10)

Paul also tells us to put on our shoes, or "whatever will make you ready" to "proclaim the gospel of peace" (Eph 6:15). It's now time for us to pull those shoes on, and pick up our satchels. A long road leads to healing and peace, but we're already on it. May God give us the strength and the courage to walk this pilgrim's way.

POSTSCRIPT

We've come a long way. We've circled through any number of healing stories, healing prayers, and healing practices. In the course of writing them, I've sat here all summer long on my benches and back deck, surrounded by dogs and cats, flowers, birds, and trees. I've written every day, through cold and rain, heat and sun. Sometimes I had no idea what was coming, but the words have always come. Although writing is a solitary business—no one telling you what to do—I've always felt you the reader in the back of my heart, waiting for something good. I hope I've given you something good, something that will help you experience peace in another way.

There's a scene I like from fourteenth century England, a scene of Julian of Norwich sitting in her small cell. Dame Julian was an anchorite—a hermit—attached to the church of St. Julian and St. Edward at Carrow. She had two windows in her cell: a 'squint' window opening into the church, and a parlor window facing the street (*Journeying,* 64). People would pass by daily, and Julian would lift a little white curtain to talk with them. I like the idea of this parlor window and curtain facing the street. There is always deep peace inside the church, but sometimes it's hidden away where people on the street can't see it. But day after day Julian sat in her room passing on parts of that peace. Maybe over her shoulder, *just there*, was a bit of shining glass or a shaft of light come down, sparkling in the eye of the passerby as Dame Julian spoke. That's what we're looking for, and that's what we see when we stop at Julian's window.

WORKS CITED

Anderson, Erica. *The Schweitzer Album*. New York: Harper & Row, 1965.

Cox, Harvey. "The Portable Sabbath" *Washington Post* 23 Oct. 1977: C1, C3.

Cunningham, Lawrence S. *The Catholic Faith: An Introduction*. New York: Paulist Press, 1987.

—. *Saint Francis of Assisi*. San Francisco: Harper & Row, 1981.

Dalai Lama, His Holiness Tenzin Gyatso the Fourteenth. *The Complete Guide to Buddhist America*. Ed. Don Morreale. Boston and London: Shambhala, 1998.

Deaner, Janice. *The Body Spoken*. New York: Dutton, 1999.

'dissolution of the monasteries.' *The Oxford Dictionary of the Christian Church*. Eds. F. L. Cross and E. A. Livingstone. Oxford: Oxford University Press, 1997.

Fénelon, François. *The Seeking Heart*. Sargent, GA: The Seed Sowers, 1992.

Garrett, George. 'Buzzard.' *Days of Our Lives Lie in Fragments*. Baton Rouge: Louisiana State University Press, 1998.

Gavitt, the Rev. Loren, ed. *Saint Augustine's Prayer Book*. West Park, NY: Holy Cross Publications, 1974.

Goodall, Jane and Marc Bekoff. *The Ten Trusts: What We Must Do to Care for the Animals We Love*. HarperSanFrancisco, 2002.

Guenther, Margaret. *The Practice of Prayer*. Boston: Cowley Publications, 1998.

Guyon, Jeanne Bouvier. *Short and Very Easy Method of Prayer. Invitation to Christian Spirituality.* Ed. John Tyson. Oxford: Oxford University Press, 1999.

Hatchett, Marion J. *Commentary on the American Prayer Book.* HarperSan-Francisco, 1995.

Heffern, Rich. 'The Ethics of Eating.' *National Catholic Reporter* 24 Jun. 2002: 7

Hildesley, C. Hugh. *Journeying with Julian.* Morehouse, 1993.

'icon.' *The Oxford Dictionary of the Christian Church.* Eds. F. L. Cross and E. A. Livingstone. Oxford: Oxford University Press, 1997.

'Iconoclastic Controversy.' *The Oxford Dictionary of the Christian Church.* Eds. F. L. Cross and E. A. Livingstone. Oxford: Oxford University Press, 1997.

Johnson, Kevin Orlin. *Rosary: Mysteries, Meditations, and the Telling of the Beads.* Dallas: Pangaeus Press, 1997.

Keating, Thomas. *Intimacy with God.* New York: Crossroad Publishing Company, 1999.

—. *Open Mind, Open Heart.* Rockport, MD: Element, 1991.

Kelsey, Morton. *Healing and Christianity.* Minneapolis: Augsburg, 1995.

Khema, Ayya. *Being Nobody, Going Nowhere.* Boston: Wisdom Publications, 1987.

Kinnell, Galway. 'Saint Francis and the Sow.' *Literature and Ourselves.* Eds. Gloria Henderson, William Day, and Sandra Waller. New York: HarperCollins College Publishers, 1994.

Nhat Hanh, Thich. *A Guide to Walking Meditation.* New Haven, CT: Eastern Press, 1985.

—. *The Miracle of Mindfulness.* Boston: Beacon Press, 1987.

—. *Touching Peace: Practicing the Art of Mindful Living.* Berkeley: Parallax Press, 1992.

'The Pilgrimage of Grace.' *The Oxford Dictionary of the Christian Church.* Eds. F. L. Cross and E. A. Livingstone. Oxford: Oxford University Press, 1997.

Saward, John. 'Berulle and the French School.' *The Study of Spirituality.* Eds. Cheslyn Jones, Geoffrey Wainwright, Edward Yarnold. Oxford: Oxford University Press, 1986.

Spearritt, Placid. 'Benedict.' *The Study of Spirituality.* Eds. Cheslyn Jones, Geoffrey Wainwright, Edward Yarnold. Oxford: Oxford University Press, 1986.

Ware, Kallistos. 'The Origins of the Jesus Prayer.' *The Study of Spirituality.* Eds. Cheslyn Jones, Geoffrey Wainwright, Edward Yarnold. Oxford: Oxford University Press, 1986.

—. 'The Spirituality of the Icon.' *The Study of Spirituality.* Eds. Cheslyn Jones, Geoffrey Wainwright, Edward Yarnold. Oxford: Oxford University Press, 1986.

Witherington III, Ben. *The Jesus Quest.* Downers Grove, IL: InterVarsity Press, 1995.

J. Ellen Nunnally is an Episcopal priest, in the Diocese of Washington, D.C., and an English professor in Ohio and Virginia. Her publications include *Foremothers: Women of the Bible*, short stories, and poetry., and she is a recipient of an Ohio Arts Council award for fiction writing. She lives in rural Ohio with her animals and family, and is an Associate of the Order of St. Helena.